e-Governance in Small States

Edited by Anthony Ming, Omer Awan and Naveed Somani

Commonwealth Secretariat

Commonwealth Secretariat
Marlborough House
Pall Mall
London SW1Y 5HX
United Kingdom

Published by the Commonwealth Secretariat
Edited by editors4change Limited
Typeset by Cenveo Publisher Services
Cover design by Tattersall, Hammarling & Silk
Printed by Hobbs the Printers, Totton, Hampshire

Views and opinions expressed in this publication are the responsibility of the authors and should in no way be attributed to the institutions to which they are affiliated or to the Commonwealth Secretariat.

Wherever possible, the Commonwealth Secretariat uses paper sourced from sustainable forests or from sources that minimise a destructive impact on the environment.

Copies of this publication may be obtained from

Publications Section
Commonwealth Secretariat
Marlborough House
Pall Mall
London SW1Y 5HX
United Kingdom
Tel: +44 (0)20 7747 6534
Fax: +44 (0)20 7839 9081
Email: publications@commonwealth.int
Web: www.thecommonwealth.org/publications

A catalogue record for this publication is available from the British Library.

ISBN (paperback): 978-1-84929-102-6
ISBN (e-book): 978-1-84859-158-5

Foreword

Small states face unique hurdles in achieving development gains such as geographic dispersion of islands, economies of scale and skills shortages. These disadvantages are well recognised. What is new and different is that there are valuable experiences concerning the ways and means of overcoming these impediments through the leveraging of information and communication technologies (ICTs) to achieve better governance, efficient and inclusive public service delivery, and social accountability.

ICTs allow for the creation of new digital pathways between citizens and governments, which are both affordable, accessible and widespread, overcoming the boundaries of time and space. This offers the opportunity for developing small states to leapfrog generations of technology when seeking to enhance governance or to deepen democracy through promoting the participation of citizens in processes that affect their lives and welfare.

Thirty-two out of the Commonwealth's fifty-four members are classified as small states, with populations of less than 1.5 million. Access and use of ICTs for governance are at a formative stage in these countries, with millions of people still outside the inclusive net of its benefits.

For such small developing countries, especially those at the nascent stage of building an e-government infrastructure, it is vital to understand where they stand in terms of their e-readiness, reflect upon the intrinsic components of an e-governance action plan, and draw lessons from the success and failures of the various e-government initiatives undertaken by other countries, developed or developing.

This book aims to strengthen the understanding of policy-makers involved in planning and execution of e-government projects, offering a helping hand by endowing them with comprehensive information about embarking successfully on the road to e-government.

It is our hope that with this knowledge, and with an early view of e-governance as not simply a technology project but as a transformative use of technology and networks to improve public sector performance and governance, policy-makers in small states can focus on developing the full potential of e-governance.

Max Everest-Phillips
Director
Governance and Institutional Development Division

Contents

List of tables, figures and boxes

Abbreviations and acronyms

C2G	citizen interactions with government
CIO	chief information officer
CSC	Community Service (or Information) Centre (India)
e-GIF	e-government interoperability framework
EGDI	E-Government Development Index
GPR	government process re-engineering
G2B	interaction between government and business
G2C	interaction between government and citizens
G2E	interaction between government and its employees
G2G	government inter-agency relationships
ICT	information and communication technology
IT	information technology
KPI	key performance indicator
NPV	net present value
NIST	US government's National Institute of Standards and Technology
OECD	Organisation for Economic Co-operation and Development
SMS	short message service (text)
UNICITRAL	UN Commission on International Trade Law
UNCTAD	UN Conference on Trade and Development
UNDP	UN Development Programme
UNESCO	UN Educational, Scientific and Cultural Organization

Summary

Though important for all governments, e-governance can play a crucial role in addressing the particular challenges faced in small states. By modernising government processes and enhancing the ability of the public sector to overcome the barriers associated with small size and isolation, e-governance can enable small state governments to cost-effectively and efficiently deliver services to their populations, as well as strengthen social accountability.

The mobilisation of information and communication technologies (ICTs) for 'micro-governance' of small developing states also improves the quality of institutions, which in turn has been shown to improve political stability, raise the public debt threshold, decrease growth volatility and increase foreign aid and investment. As government is often the largest business and economic player in small states, the move towards e-governance will have a far larger impact and ripple effect on the country's economic and social development than one would see in larger or developed countries. It is therefore a key tool to further economic development and good governance in small states.

However, small states face considerable challenges in developing e-governance, including the high cost of technology, the lack of infrastructure, limited human capital and a weak private sector. Eighteen of the Commonwealth's thirty-two small state member countries are ranked in the bottom half of e-government indices.

This book was motivated by a desire to leverage e-governance lessons in Commonwealth countries and small states in order to maximise the success of future country initiatives. Recognising that there is no 'one size fits all' e-governance solution, it outlines the essential elements and prerequisites for e-governance in small states for use by policy-makers and government officials who are responsible for or associated with managing e-governance projects in small states.

One fundamental theme of the book is that e-governance is not a technology project; it is a government transformation project. It is not merely the computerisation of government operations, but a process that supports fundamental elements of good governance such as democracy, democratic processes and institutions that reflect fundamental human rights, openness, participation and effective, just and honest government.

E-government tools should be linked to wider good governance goals. As such, like any government reform effort, significant political will is required for its success. E-governance should not be led by technicians but by policy-makers, and a strong political champion for e-governance is essential. Leaders must understand how to customise applications to policy goals, in concert with how to revamp underlying business processes and organisational structures and capacities, and with an understanding of the importance of data standards and architecture for systems interoperability. This book thus familiarises policy-makers with the processes involved and 'best fit' practices in e-governance from a small state perspective.

Chapter 1 provides an outline of e-government and e-governance, including an overview of their potential benefits, a description of ICT and e-government strategies, an e-governance framework and an explanation of the stages of maturity of e-governance.

Chapter 2 outlines how challenges faced in common by small states – including isolation, susceptibility to natural disasters and income volatility, and limited institutional capacity – can be mitigated and managed through the use of ICTs in government operations and practices. It provides a framework of the specific prerequisite conditions essential for e-governance success in small states.

Aligning ICTs with a well-developed strategy that addresses a country's own economic, social and transformational needs and goals will leverage this critical resource to provide more citizen-centric services. **Chapter 3** outlines the e-government strategy development process, highlighting good practices in terms of leadership, corporate governance, consultation and strategy development, financing, and monitoring and evaluation.

The potential of e-government to improve efficiency, citizen-centricity, transparency and accountability will not necessarily be delivered until public sector processes are reconfigured and redesigned. Government process re-engineering (GPR), explained in **Chapter 4**, is a methodology for the analysis and redesign of organisational processes. However, as a process of change, e-governance and GPR must be accompanied by appropriate leadership, as well as strategies for change management and communication, in order to succeed.

E-governance is an iterative process; plans and strategies must be updated to reflect new government priorities and innovative technologies. An approach to the attainment of e-governance should therefore be designed as multi-pronged from the outset of the implementation process. **Chapter 5** elaborates key steps in the successful implementation of e-governance, including the development of legislative, regulatory and policy components, ICT architecture and standards, and ICT infrastructure.

In the implementation of e-government applications, cost and reach are paramount concerns to ensure sustainability and impact. **Chapter 6** explores emerging directions in e-governance that are of particular relevance to small states. The rapid growth as well as the affordability, usability and mobility of mobile technology herald the importance of 'm-governance' as a service delivery channel and a tool to strengthen citizen–state relationships. Moreover, the need to reduce the capital costs associated with e-government has also led to the increased use of cloud services within and outside government.

E-government catalyses the public service so that it can achieve its broader goals. E-government is thus a tool, a facilitator and an enabler, rather than an end in itself. As the public sector reforms structural processes and institutions for greater efficiency and better service delivery, creates institutional inter-linkages between government and offers greater participation for citizens, e-governance will increasingly become a key enabler of sustainable development and democracy in small states.

About the authors

Mr Anthony Ming is ICT Advisor at the Commonwealth Secretariat and is responsible for implementing technology-related mandates issued by Commonwealth Heads of Government. He provides strategic and policy advice to 54 member countries in high priority development areas such as e-/m-governance, national ICT strategies, government process re-engineering, ICT in education and strategic partnership development.

Prior to joining the Commonwealth Secretariat in 2008, Tony occupied a series of senior management positions in the Ontario Government and was responsible for implementing enterprise-wide ICT initiatives. Tony was part of the Ontario Government Management Team created to negotiate a collective agreement with the largest union in the Province. During 2006–2007 Tony returned to his country of birth, Guyana, to re-engineer the Revenue Authority and manage the implementation of the value added tax, customs and excise and other tax systems.

Tony lectured at York University, Toronto, Canada for over 20 years on a variety of topics including information and communications technology, project management, accounting and finance. He is Managing Editor for the Taylor and Francis journal *Information Technology for Development*.

Mr Omer A Awan has been a Programme Officer at the Commonwealth Secretariat since 2008. He has extensive research and project management experience in the area of ICT4Development and e-/m-governance and has carried out research in areas such as: ICTs and access to education, ICTs and human capital enrichment, pre-requisites of e-governance, potential of e-/m-governance in bringing citizens closer to governments, and the role of international organisations in promoting e-governance.

Prior to joining Commonwealth Secretariat, he worked as Assistance Professor & Research Associate at Iqra University, Islamabad, Pakistan. He worked as a Functional Consultant on the World Bank's Project to Improve Financial Reporting and Auditing (PIFRA) in Pakistan. He holds MSc in Poverty Reduction & Development Management from the University of Birmingham as well as MBA and BBA (Hons) degrees.

Mr David Spiteri Gingell has held a series of high level appointments with the Government of Malta including: Chairman and Chief Executive Officer of the Malta Information Technology Agency; Chief Executive Officer of Enemalta Corporation; Executive Chairman of the Malta Council for Science and Technology (MCST); Chairman of EuroMedITI Ltd; and Chief Information Management Officer for the Public Service. David played a key role in the design and implementation of public service reform between 1990 and 2000 in his respective capacity as Director of the Consultancy Division within MSU Ltd and the Management Efficiency Unit within the Office of the Prime Minister.

In April 2008, David established David Spiteri Gingell Consulting – incorporated as DSG Consulting Ltd in September 2011.

David holds a BA (Hons) in Public Administration from the University of Malta and a Master's degree in Public Administration (with distinction) from the University of Liverpool, UK. David was bestowed the Order of the Terra Mariana by the President of Estonia in 2001.

Mr Naveed Somani has been an ICT researcher with the Commonwealth Secretariat since late 2011. His research has covered a variety of topics including ICTs and corruption, e-government 2.0, and the role of international organisations in promoting e-government. His work with small states has taken him to the Caribbean, Mauritius and the Pacific, working on ICT in education initiatives and the development of national ICT strategies. Prior to joining the Secretariat, he worked with a humanitarian relief charity focusing on ICT-related projects including mobile banking initiatives, satellite/SMS early-warning systems and humanitarian accountability software systems. He holds a Bachelor's degree in Jurisprudence from the University of Oxford and a Master's degree in International Studies and Development from the School of Oriental and African Studies.

Ms Maryam Amin is currently teaching modules of ICT4Development, public policy and e-government as visiting faculty in Pakistan and has considerable research experience in this area. She has previously worked in Pakistan's NGO sector. She holds a Master's degree in Public Administration from the London School of Economics and a Bachelor's degree in Development Studies.

Ms Katherine Kirkby worked as Research Intern at the Commonwealth Secretariat. She has extensive research experience in the areas of public health, international development and e-governance. She holds a Master's degree in Global Health Science from Oxford University and a Bachelor's Degree in Anthropology and Development Studies from the University of Sussex.

Chapter 1

Introduction to e-Governance

Omer Awan, Maryam Amin and Katherine Kirkby

1.1 Defining e-government and e-governance

The emergence of the internet and other information and communication technologies (ICTs) has drastically altered traditional service delivery methods and interactions within government and its stakeholders. The expectation is now of services being delivered with greater efficiency and accessibility, and within a shorter time frame. This brings forth the initiative of e-government, which is primarily concerned with the use of ICTs by government agencies to electronically deliver their services (Patel and Jacobson 2008). Now e-government has become an imperative and unavoidable phenomenon in contemporary public administration.

E-government can be described as the use of information technologies to transform relations with citizens, businesses and other sectors of government. It can serve a multitude of purposes including better delivery of government services to citizens; improved communication with business and industry; citizen empowerment through access to information; and more competent government management (World Bank 2005, cited by Dada 2006). According to Abramson and Means (2001), e-government can be defined as the electronic interaction (transaction and information exchange) between the government, the public (citizens and businesses) and employees. Moreover, e-government has been defined as the transformation of the public sector's internal and external relationships through net-enabled operations and ICT, in order to improve government service delivery and citizen participation (Fraga 2002). According to World Bank (2001:1), e-government is the 'government owned or operated systems of information and information technologies that transform relations with citizens, the private sector and/or other government agencies so as to promote citizens' empowerment, improve service delivery, strengthen accountability, increase transparency, or improve government efficiency'.

E-governance is the utilisation of information and communications technology to interact with and provide services to businesses, citizens and other governments with the intent to improve transparency, increase public service efficiency and deepen democracy.

Various terms besides 'e-government' are used to describe this phenomenon of ICT usage by the government, such as 'e-governance', 'online government', 'one-stop government' and 'digital government' (Andersen and Henriksen 2006). While 'government' represents a 'superstructure that deals with decisions, rules, implementation and outputs of its policies' (UNPA and ASPA 2001), 'governance' refers to operations conducted on the basis of processes, objectives, performance, co-ordination and outcomes. Moreover, e-governance is based on four processes – namely, electronic consultation, electronic controllership, electronic engagement and networked societal guidance – whereas e-government refers to the structure that is responsible for electronic service delivery, electronic workflow, electronic voting and electronic productivity. E-governance is the public sector's use of the most innovative information and communication technologies, such as the internet, to deliver to all citizens improved services, reliable information and greater knowledge in order to facilitate access to the governing process and encourage deeper citizen participation (UNPA and ASPA 2001). According to Saxena (2005), e-governance is the outcome of 'effects produced' by public administration, whereas e-government refers to the outputs of 'efforts expended' by the public administration; thus, e-government is apparently a subset of e-governance (ibid).

E-governance aims to make the interaction between government and citizens (G2C), government and its employees (G2E), government and business enterprises (G2B) and inter-agency relationships (G2G) more friendly, convenient, transparent and inexpensive. The goals of e-governance are:

- better service delivery to citizens;

- enhanced transparency and accountability;

- empowering people through information;

- improved efficiency within governments; and

- improved interface with business and industry (NISG 2012).

The above definitions, as well as others, place emphasis on the definition of e-government as primarily the leveraging of new technology channels to transform the way government interacts with society at large, be this with regards to information, service delivery transactions, or the strengthening of democracy through increased transparency and accountability – more recently referred to as 'e-democracy and e-governance'. In essence, e-government is seen as a new means of reforming the way government and its institutions behave.

However, this is argued to be a narrow view of e-government from the perspective of state development. In small and island states, as well as in developing countries, government is usually the largest 'business' and economic player in society. Policy decisions taken by a government perpetually have a far larger impact and ripple effect on a country's development than one would see in larger and developed countries. Specifically with regards to e-government, a decision by a government to adopt a strategy to implement e-government should be seen beyond the confines of a transformation of the way public institutions deliver services and are held accountable. Rather, e-government provides the platform and the drive to secure further economic and social development through an information society and an information economy.

1.2 Why e-governance? – Linking ICTs with governance

In recent years, e-governance has proved itself to be the new path to improvement and success for the public sectors of both developed and developing countries (Dada 2006). It is also credited as having the ability to decrease poverty and corruption (UNDP 2005; Dada 2006; Coursey and Norris 2008) In the case of national and local governments, it is referred to as a source for better service delivery, increasing participation, sustainable development, democracy, transparency and accountability, greater accessibility, growth of revenue and/or cost reductions, and for improved communication between citizens and government in the form of more efficient and responsive national institutions (ibid). There are many successful case studies regarding the role of e-governance and ICTs in achieving such goals. The following subsection will highlight some of the case studies, with reference to the basic pillars of governance.

1.2.1 ICTs and increased transparency

ICTs enable the provision of prompt and transparent information online, as well as the creation of visual or analytic tools that simplify complex information. Transparency portals developed by governments around the world provide free and open access to government information and spending, thus promoting public accountability, decreasing corruption and developing a sense of citizen ownership over government spending priorities (Fung et al. 2010). Other non-governmental websites, such as the Budget Tracking Tool in Kenya, enable citizen monitoring of government spending to help to combat corruption. The Commonwealth Secretariat has developed a similar initiative in Sierra Leone, the Transparency Sierra Leone Portal (TSL-P), a dynamic gateway where government records, spanning the full panoply of government activities, are made public. The portal itself focuses on three key aspects of open governance: accountability, engagement and collaboration. It does this by serving as the access point for three key sites: the Government of Sierra Leone (GoSL) Intranet, Project Tracker and Join Our Transformation. The first of these is the GoSL Intranet, which provides a collaborative space where various ministries can interact and search for content, in addition to being the central dashboard for all performance reports. As well as improving internal governance, the intranet will also act as an engine for the portal, constantly providing material that can be deposited onto the TSL-P for public scrutiny. The Project Tracker is the primary method through which users track the implementation of 'Agenda for Change' projects. Links to reports include key data such as project cost, contractor details and implementation timelines. By building a reliable evidence base citizens act as virtual watchdogs, ensuring their rights are protected, projects are delivered as promised and officials are held to account when funds are misspent. The 'Join Our Transformation' (JOT) site harnesses the full potential of Web 2.0 technologies to encourage a national debate on the government's poverty reduction strategy. Combining authoritative content with community-created content, it establishes a deliberative space where discussions can move from service delivery issues, to addressing larger transformational concerns.

However, creating such websites is one step: citizens must also be able to access, understand and use this information. Adequate ICT infrastructure, broadband access and digital literacy are some prerequisite conditions. Community Information Centres in India have improved access to information and to a variety of public services via kiosks in villages all over the country. This has not only facilitated access in rural areas and decreased corruption, but has also has resulted in significant economic gains for local people.

Box 1.1 Transparency Portal (Brazil)

Brazil's Transparency Portal is a general gateway where budgetary information is presented in a user-friendly format and updated daily. Citizen awareness of the portal and how to use it was promoted. Citizens can interact with the portal's team through surveys, and can report misconducts and crimes through a whistle-blower channel.

Impact: The portal has received international awards, including being recognised by the UN Office on Drugs and Crime (UNODC) as one of the five best initiatives in the world related to corruption prevention. The number of citizens accessing the portal has grown from 10,000 to 260,000 per month, and the media has made extensive use of the website in order to investigate corruption schemes and frauds involving federal resources (Sobrinh 2011). Regional neighbours such as Peru, Bolivia and Chile have launched their own transparency portals, as have countries throughout Africa and Asia – including recently Sierra Leone, with support from the Commonwealth Secretariat.

Box 1.2 The Budget Tracking Tool (Kenya)

Constituency Development Fund (CDF) money has been controversial in Kenya because it is under the control of Members of Parliament (MPs); there have been many instances of misuse and theft. The Budget Tracking Tool is a collaborative platform that allows citizens to view projects and expenditures of the CDF, allowing grassroots communities to see whether MPs are following through on their promises (Heacock 2010).

Impact: The system gets 5,700 short message service (SMS) and web queries per month about development projects, and citizens have used the information obtained to expose corruption at local as well as national levels of government. One example was the uncovering of a major corruption scandal at the Ministry of Water, which led to the firing of a number of public officials involved.

Box 1.3 Community Information Centres (India)

Community Services Centres (CSCs) are delivery points for multiple government, private and social sector services to rural citizens in India, who otherwise have to face logistical and financial costs to access such services. CSCs are run by a local entrepreneur, who can generate income from users.

Impact: As of 30 April 2012, a total of 88,995 CSCs were operational in 33 states. One hundred per cent of CSCs have been rolled out in twelve states (UNESCO 2005). CSCs charge users nominal amounts for services, yet substantive revenue generation has been achieved by many, and this pays the salaries of operators and supports sustainability. Keeping in view the scope of the project in terms of its coverage and scope of services offered to citizens, it has created an immense impact in terms of effective service delivery to rural areas of India.

1.2.2 ICTs and improving public service delivery through monitoring and feedback

Improving the access and quality of public services is a political, social and economic imperative for all developing countries. Through the World Development Report 2004, the World Bank highlighted that too often services fail the poor, and recommended that in order to improve service delivery, institutions need to be developed that strengthen the accountability relationship between policy-makers, service providers and citizens.

A key route to improving the availability, quality and responsiveness of public services is to augment citizen monitoring and feedback (Gaventa 2010). The following case studies illustrate how water, education and health service delivery can be made transparent and accountable by empowering stakeholders with information and monitoring tools.

Box 1.4 Raising the Water Pressure (Tanzania)

More than half of Tanzania's rural water points are malfunctioning, despite increases in government funding and population growth, and less than half of new funding was going to wards with below average coverage of water facilities. In a citizen survey in 2008, water supply was identified by citizens as one of the top three priorities for government to address. The 'Raising the Water Pressure' programme enables citizens in rural areas to send feedback or grievances about their local water supply through their mobile phones. This information is forwarded to the appropriate district officials and the local media. Local media can then interact with district officials to determine their plan of action regarding the poor water service.

Impact: As of 2011, 18,829 texts had been sent to the water database, information which was used to get 12 water points in 3 districts repaired, improving water access to up to 24,000 people. The programme has created incentives for government to be more responsive to citizens and deliver services. As a result of its success, a similar initiative is being developed for the education and health sectors (Daraja 2011).

Box 1.5 Stop Stockouts (Kenya and Uganda)

The 'Stop Stockouts' campaign lobbies African governments to meet their obligations to provide essential medicines by increasing the national budgetary allocation for the purchase of these medicines, and by ensuring efficiency and transparency in the procurement, supply and distribution of medicines.

Stop Stockouts uses FrontlineSMS technology in its monitoring activities – such as 'Pill Checks', where researchers visit public health institutions to check on the availability of essential medicines. Stop Stockouts states that FrontlineSMS technology has greatly improved its communications, reducing time spent, and enabling online mapping of results for easy comprehension and sharing. The results have been highly impactful, and governments are also currently using SMS to collect their own data and monitor facilities.

Source: http://stopstockouts.org (accessed 22 March 2013).

Box 1.6 CU@SCHOOL (Uganda)

Teachers' absenteeism in Uganda is one of the highest in the world, with rates of 20–30 per cent, costing the government US$30 million every year and with obvious implications for the quality of education. In addition, 27 per cent of Ugandan children are not in school at any given moment, despite free universal education (Twawesa 2010). Despite these dramatic figures, no routine data is available on pupil and teacher attendance.

The CU@SCHOOL pilot project uses mobile phones to monitor teacher and pupil attendance and absenteeism in 100 primary schools on a weekly basis. This information is mapped and sent to newspapers and radio shows, school management and district officials. Mobile phone coverage is exceptional in Uganda: almost one in three people own a phone, and mobile networks reach 90 per cent of the country. Provided the pilot is successful, measured using a randomised control trial methodology, the aim is to integrate the use of mobile technology into Uganda's new Education Management Information System. The information will support short-, medium- and long-term planning.

Box 1.7 E-governance in Seychelles

In 2012 the United Nations Public Administration Network's e-government index ranked Seychelles as number one in the African region. Citizens in Seychelles can now interact with and obtain government services in the comfort of their homes through the use of information and communications technology (ICT).

The Commonwealth Secretariat provided a comprehensive package of assistance consisting of strategy and policy formulation; capacity building in key areas such as service management and government process re-engineering; and hands-on advice to implement some of these processes. The assistance provided by the Secretariat resulted in a big picture view of e-government, clarity on the way forward, building sustainable capacity development and robust implementation support. E-government is not a technology project but a government transformation initiative. Seychelles now has a clear understanding of the importance of re-engineering ineffective processes and how to achieve this using technology.

Sustainability

Seychelles developed a robust training programme to build the in-house capacity required to sustain the e-government platform, and encouraged the spread of ICT knowledge by providing subsidised laptop computers to high school students. The ICT department partnered with the Ministry of Finance to secure funding for the programme and its maintenance. To sustain and continue with the programme, Seychelles built strategic partnerships with international organisations and the private sector to provide additional support and resources.

1.2.3 ICTs and increasing citizen-led government accountability and responsiveness

Participation is defined as 'a process through which stakeholders influence and share control over development initiatives and the decisions and resources which affect them' (World Bank 1994). Citizen engagement and participation has been evidenced to increase civic and political knowledge, foster a greater sense of empowerment, deepen networks, increase access to state services and resources, and enhance state responsiveness (Gaventa and Barret 2010). However, to allow for a more equitable development process, disadvantaged stakeholders need to be empowered to increase their level of knowledge, influence and control over their own livelihoods, including development initiatives affecting them.

ICTs can facilitate both transparency and participation in public service delivery, which can lead to increases in efficiency and responsiveness, as well as improvements in the government's ability to correctly prioritise government services to correspond with citizen desires. Not only can public trust in government be enhanced, but inclusion and empowerment of groups often excluded from the policy process can be increased through extension of information access and capability to all citizens, as evidenced by the ICT4GOV programme in the DR Congo (see Box 1.8).

Mobile phones have enabled 'crowdsourcing', or the gathering of information from large numbers of people, which can help to solve potential problems ranging from public service delivery issues to election riots or crime. Ushahidi used crowdsourcing to enable citizens to provide quick geo-referenced information during elections to mobilise government help (see Box 1.9). The mobility, ease of use, flexible deployment and affordability of wireless technologies enables their use by citizens even in rural populations with low levels of income and literacy, as well as their adaptation to a variety of applications.

Moreover, developing countries look upon e-governance as a new way to increase their involvement in the world economy through the production and distribution of new information and knowledge products (UNDP 2005). The global market for ICT services and ICT-enabled services is large and growing, creating new opportunities for economic growth, social empowerment and grassroots innovation in developing countries. Through building an appropriate legal and regulatory framework and developing ICT infrastructure, an environment can be created where the private sector, communities and individuals can make the most of ICTs in all areas of society. There is also a direct impact on the economy, as in the case of e-procurement, which creates wider competition and more participants in the public sector marketplace.

ICTs can also be utilised to promote new solutions for existing development challenges. For example, technology has been used to reduce social exclusion by providing residents of deprived and remote areas with access to the same services and information that were only previously available to the residents of privileged areas. In this way, e-governance acts as a spur towards the building of an ICT-enriched human capital- and knowledge-based society by diffusing technology and bridging digital divides.

Box 1.8 ICT4GOV (DR Congo)

With the support of the World Bank, the Congolese government launched an ICT for Governance (ICT4GOV) pilot programme in 2009 in South Kivu province, which suffered from years of civil conflict, political instability, mismanagement and corruption. The initiative aimed to facilitate decentralisation by empowering stakeholders to participate in the process of ICT-based participatory budgeting. Citizens were enabled to vote via SMS or at voting stations on a shortlist of budget priorities for the district, as well as to receive updates about how the budget was allocated and to give feedback about the project's implementation.

Impact: In some areas, more than US$80,000 was invested in interventions such as school building, health clinics, roads or irrigation structures; in most cases, this was the first time that any real investment was made in the districts. For instance, Ibanda, a rural community, went from not having any investment budget to having 40 per cent of its budget devoted to investments. Levels of local tax collection have increased following the process, suggesting that citizens became more willing to pay their taxes as they believed that government would actually use their tax dollars to deliver services (World Bank 2012). The programme is now being scaled-up country wide.

Box 1.9 Ushahidi (Kenya)

Following the post-election crisis in Kenya, there was a need to accurately and efficiently monitor election fraud and rioting in order to mobilise support to prevent or mitigate such situations. Ushahidi created a crowdsourcing information and internet-mapping site that allowed users to submit eye-witness accounts of election fraud and riots via web, email, text or Twitter, in order to help mobilise support for preventing or mitigating crisis situations. Information sent via SMS or through the media was verified, mapped for the public to view online and communicated to public authorities, which could respond to the reports.

Impact: Between 30 December 2007 and 1 April 2008, the platform had 45,000 unique visits, 173,000 page views and 220 incident reports (Hanna 2012). Ushahidi is often cited as an example of how mobile phones provide a good complement to government-led governance. The platform has been deployed in other countries, including Uchaguzi in Uganda, Sudan Vote Monitor, Cuidemos el Voto in Mexico, Eleitor2010 in Brazil and Amatora mu Mahoro in Burundi. Furthermore, the platform has been adapted for other reporting objectives, such as a child violence reporting programme in Benin, and Stop Stockouts' 'Pill Check Week' in countries around Africa.

Moreover, according to Ciborra (2005) the improved perceptions of good governance and increased development that arise from implementing e-governance initiatives lead to small and developing states benefitting as recipients of increased aid from richer, larger and more developed nations (Dada 2006).

Such case studies show how e-governance initiatives contribute to increasing state responsiveness, the lowering of corruption, building new democratic spaces for citizen engagement and empowering local voices. However, they also reveal how transparency does not automatically lead to greater social accountability and better governance. Any conclusions on the impact of transparency and accountability initiatives must also be located within a broader discussion of the contexts within which these occur, as context affects which transparency or accountability initiatives are feasible, the internal effectiveness of initiatives, and their interaction with broader external factors (McGee and Gaventa 2010).

1.3 Complexity of e-governance – is it all about ICTs?

The case studies mentioned above highlight how e-governance initiatives contribute to increasing state responsiveness, lowering of corruption, building new democratic spaces for citizen engagement and empowering local voices. However, they also reveal how transparency does not automatically lead to greater social accountability and better governance. Any conclusions on the impact of transparency and accountability initiatives must also be located within a broader discussion of the contexts within which these occur, as context affects which transparency or accountability initiatives are feasible, the internal effectiveness of initiatives and their interaction with broader external factors (McGee and Gaventa 2010). Nonetheless, through such case study research it is possible to identify lessons in terms of the enabling conditions that support the development and implementation of successful e-governance.

Although it has been considered that e-governance is all about the application of ICTs in the public sector, the overall process is much more complex and requires multiple factors to be taken into account. It is due to such ignorance that although an estimated US$3 trillion was spent during the first decade of the twenty-first century on government information systems (Gubbins 2004), recent studies suggest between 60 and 80 per cent of e-government projects fail in some way leading to 'a massive wastage of financial, human and political resources, and an inability to deliver the potential benefits of e-governance to its beneficiaries' (Heeks 2006: 3).

The complexity of the e-governance can be determined by the following key challenges and external factors, which play an important role in the success and failure of e-governance interventions (see Chapter 3 for further details).

1.3.1 Political commitment and responsiveness
E-governance implies changes in the culture of government and how it relates to citizens as clients, requiring not only citizen participation but also the ability and

incentives of the public sector to listen to citizens and respond to feedback. To this end, secure political commitment and technical competencies to engage citizens, manage change and open government, leverage social networks, and integrate knowledge from multiple participants, is central to most e-governance initiatives (Hanna 2012). Without political will, transparency – including the creation of transparency portals or the provision of open data – is difficult. Initiatives such as the Budget Tracking Tool in Kenya have experienced challenges due to inaccessibility of public data (Heacock 2010).

However, even the existence of committed political leaders may not be enough to bring about desired changes if there are structural constraints, such as lack of financial and political autonomy to carry out reforms or take action against corrupt officials (McGee and Gaventa 2010). Therefore, it is also essential that there exist mechanisms and resources for government to act based on citizen feedback, citizen demands or corruption allegations.

1.3.2 Capabilities and motivation for citizen participation

If citizens are not able to process, analyse or use information gained from greater transparency initiatives, such information cannot be used effectively. These capabilities can be strengthened by a number of factors, including increased access (e.g. Community Information Centres in India); an active media (e.g. 'Raising the Water Pressure' in Tanzania); social mobilisation; the existence of coalitions and 'infomediaries' (Hanna 2012). It is also important to adapt e-governance initiatives to education level, culture, language, gender and other characteristics, as well as to facilitate participation through decreasing the costs (time, money, uncertainty, insecurity) and increasing the benefits (rewards, change and capacity building) of such participation (Murillo 2012).

The approach and focus of e-governance initiatives should be tailored to the specific country context, including the types, motives, incentives and capabilities of potential users – both citizens (who can provide feedback on improving public services) and organisations or journalists (who are better positioned in some ways to put pressure on government) (Hanna 2012). A number of studies show that transparency and accountability mechanisms gain more traction when linked to other mobilisation strategies, such as advocacy, litigation, electoral pressure or protest movements (McGee and Gaventa 2010).

1.3.3 ICT infrastructure

The effectiveness of e-governance initiatives in reaching citizens and businesses depends greatly on the availability of ICT infrastructure, including connectivity and broadband penetration and access. Mobile telephony, wireless access and other technological options should be explored by policy-makers with regard to coverage and cost, with the recognition that strategic e-governance may be a key catalyst in reaching development targets and equitable public services for remote communities (McGee and Gaventa 2010).

As demonstrated in the case studies, a variety of ICT tools can be applied to increase capacity building, curb corruption and improve public service delivery. These include websites (e.g. transparency portals), crowdsourcing and geospatial technologies (e.g. Ushahidi or Stop Stockouts), kiosks (e.g. CSCs in India) and mobile devices (e.g. 'Raising the Water Pressure' or ICT4GOV). Tools need to be chosen in terms of their suitability, accessibility, affordability, mobility and user-friendliness. Rather than using ICT tools in isolation, ICT technologies can be fused within initiatives to maximise citizen participation (Kuriyan et al. 2011).

1.3.4 Organisational partnerships

In all the case studies, organisational partnerships were a key ingredient for success. Such initiatives require partnerships between government, policy-makers, regulators, network operators and service providers, hardware manufacturers, content providers, application developers, the media, donors and civil society (Hanna 2012). Civil society in particular can facilitate the implementation of large-scale projects to less accessible areas and at the grassroots level (UNESCO 2007), while telecommunications companies or ICT specialists can help in the implementation of projects, such as Airtel in the DR Congo case study (Box 1.8).

Many of the case study initiatives worked with the media in order to inform citizens about initiatives – for instance, in the initiation of the Transparency Portal in Brazil – and to publicise the findings or feedback gained from the initiatives – for instance, in 'Raising the Water Pressure' in Tanzania to increase pressure on government. A free media is also therefore an important component for the success of open government initiatives.

1.3.5 Sustainability

Many e-governance tools and initiatives are funded by external donors or government budgets and for specific periods of time. After the expiry period, there is a risk that these initiatives may come to a standstill. This was evidenced in ICT electoral tools such as the Ugandan Election Watch 2011 and Uchaguzi (Hanna 2012). This not only raises the problem of measuring their impact, but can also sour citizens' appetite for engaging with similar tools in the future (World Bank 2012). There may also be too many of the same types of platforms created by various organisations, leading to a duplication of efforts and citizen confusion. Sustainability needs to be an intention of ICT initiatives right from the start and should be designed into the initiative (Gaventa and Barrett 2010). Consistent political commitment is one way to increase sustainability, exemplified by the commitment of the Brazilian government to constantly improving its Transparency Portal, as is increasing the self-sufficiency of e-governance tools, such as the locally-owned, revenue-producing CSCs in India.

1.4 Governance before e-governance

E-governance is a tool, a facilitator and an enabler for government change and improvement, rather than an end in itself. It catalyses the public service, so that it can achieve its broader goals.

Governance is the outcome of the interaction of government, the public service and citizens throughout the political process, policy development, programme design and service delivery. E-governance supports fundamental elements of good governance such as: democracy, democratic processes and institutions that reflect national circumstances; fundamental human rights, the rule of law and independence of the judiciary; effective, just and honest government; openness and participation; inclusiveness; accountability and effectiveness. Good fit governance goals dictate the design and share of e-tools for improving governance outcomes and processes. The purpose of implementing e-governance is to improve governance processes and outcomes with a view to improving the delivery of public services to citizens. Commitment to governance issues and a good governance model must therefore precede the development of e-governance.

E-governance is not a 'quick-fix' solution; the journey to attain e-governance is generational, requiring various stages of maturity. It is also an iterative process, as plans and strategies have to be updated to reflect new government priorities and innovative technologies. It therefore requires both short-term strategies and long-term planning.

The importance of the planning stage of e-governance cannot be stressed enough. Technology needs to be adapted to government needs and local context, and incorporated into existing strategies for change.

As the public sector draws upon technologies to reform structural processes and institutions for greater efficiency and better service delivery, it is essential for there to be a deep understanding of the structures, relationships, institutional spaces, interests and incentives that underpin current processes (IDS 2010) before applying e-tools. Policy-makers should be alert to ways in which the design of public programmes, including e-governance initiatives, influences opportunities and incentives for collective action.

1.5 Developing e-governance initiatives – two basic pillars

1.5.1 National ICT strategy

A crucial prerequisite for the realisation of ICTs for governance is the creation of a coherent national ICT strategy that integrates ICTs with national development plans and conceives a policy framework in which to embed various public sector reform initiatives. National ICT strategies are important in that they:

*   elevate ICT for development as a priority;

*   link ICT to the achievement of a country's national policies and, at a global level, to the Millennium Development Goals (MDGs);

*   generate economic growth and create job opportunities;

- create a roadmap to chart the course for a well-orchestrated introduction of large ICT investments; and

- provide a coherent framework for utilising ICTs in multiple sectors to facilitate efficient public service delivery and develop a knowledge-based society.

A national ICT strategy is also necessary to obtain government/political buy-in. Governments require long implementation timeframes and extensive multi-stakeholder consultations. Although national ICT strategic development is a comprehensive process, there are two common stages/prerequisites for the development of such a strategy:

a) **E-readiness.** Before embarking on the design of a national ICT strategy, a country should refer to the results of an e-readiness assessment – of which there are numerous definitions. Generally 'e-readiness' depends upon an assessment of the current level of ICT sophistication, including infrastructure, industry competitiveness, skills development, the legal and regulatory environment, and e-government initiatives already underway. E-readiness assessments often include a SWOT (strengths, weaknesses, opportunities, threats) analysis of the ICT sector, as well as a collection of primary and secondary data for internationally and nationally recognised indicators.

    However, according to Veizi and Bimar (2009) an 'e-ready' society is one that has: the necessary physical infrastructure (high bandwidth, reliability and affordable prices); integrated current ICTs throughout businesses (e-commerce, local ICT sector), communities (local content, many organisations online, ICTs used in every-day life, ICTs taught in schools) and the government (e-government); strong telecommunications competition; independent regulation with a commitment to universal access; and no limits on trade or foreign investment.

    Various international organisations, such as the UN, World Bank and Economics Intelligence Unit, carry out e-readiness surveys and publish rankings to assist countries in identifying their current standings in the sectors mentioned above.

b) **Benchmarking.** Based on e-readiness assessments, a government needs to set targets – or benchmark. Benchmarking defines the gap between the current and future state, and thus informs the development of a roadmap to move a country towards the future state. ICT baseline indicators (international rankings, reference countries, best practices/centres of excellence) are used to track progress to achieving goals.

    Following this, a roadmap is created with the aim of bridging the gap – the national ICT strategy. This roadmap does not focus only on IT infrastructure; rather a coherent and well-established national ICT strategy provides a holistic overview of linkages between using ICTs in achieving national development goals including education, health and agriculture etc. The strategy includes resource and funding requirements and sources for sustainability, as well as a monitoring, evaluation and reporting mechanism. It sets out pathfinder projects, or starting projects, which will be implemented to demonstrate progress and build momentum.

A typical, well-developed national ICT strategy covers multiple areas, and also depends on the development goals and priorities of specific countries. However, there are certain common key considerations in the design of a coherent and well-targeted national ICT strategy. These include:

- producing and using ICTs for social and economic advantage;

- developing human resources for effective national ICT strategies;

- promoting and financing investment in ICTs;

- creating and accessing scientific and technical knowledge;

- managing ICTs for development – linking ICTs with national development goals (e-business, e-learning, e-health, e-employment, e-environment, e-agriculture and e-science); and

- e-governance – focus on improving the effectiveness and transparency of public administration activities by making use of ICT in government-to-government, government-to-citizen and government-to-business relations (Crede and Mansell 1998; ITU 2011).

The approval and commitment of senior executives in government, as well as other stakeholders, is essential for buy-in and success of the strategy. To achieve this, establishing a senior minister as a strong sponsor for the initiative and identifying champions within each ministry has been shown to be a successful tactic. Moreover, broad national engagement involving government, industry, and academic and civil society is a must. The national ICT strategy should be viewed and positioned as a national development initiative – not as a government IT initiative. It should also be directly linked to national goals and development objectives.

1.5.2 E-governance strategy

All developing countries have introduced, and many have successfully implemented, e-government visions and strategies. Once a more comprehensive national ICT strategy is in place, which also covers the investment in basic ICT infrastructure as well as a roadmap for ICT development in the country, developing a strategic plan for e-governance is essential for leaders to guide their ministries. Strategic planning efforts are useful because they help the government to develop a vision of how to deploy e-governance services and a roadmap to follow to deliver services. The goal of the e-governance strategic plan is to ensure that managers have a clear approach for managing the ICT department, in spite of their limited knowledge of ICT. The plan develops an inventory of the computing needs of each department, categorises the components of the ICT infrastructure, provides guidance on how to protect the security and emergency management of all ICT-enabled services, and creates a timetable to integrate fragmented application programmes into enterprise architecture (ITU 2008).

Undoubtedly each country's strategy is driven by its own value system, as well as political, social and economic drivers. A study carried out by Parisopoluous et al. (2007) that analysed e-government strategies introduced in the European Union, identified 29 main objectives that are usually pursued by e-government strategies and refer to a wide spectrum of e-government aspects at all levels: government-to-citizen (G2C), government-to-business (G2B) and government-to-government (G2G). The design of the e-governance strategy reflects the level of maturity of a country's ability to implement e-governance; therefore, the scope and number of objectives varies. Having said that, there are ten strategic objectives that reappear in most of the strategies studied (see Box 1.10). This shows that the compelling drivers that lead nations to design holistic e-governance strategies and embark on comprehensive implementation programmes tend to be consistent. They are compelling reasons for the adoption of an e-governance strategy, irrespective of whether they are applied to advanced or developing small states.

Box 1.10 Common strategic objectives

1. The set-up of a single access point (portal) in order to deliver e-government services

2. The enhancement of ICT skills, both for civil employees and society in general

3. The guaranteed trust, transparency and accountability of government, privacy and security for transactions with government

4. The delivery of public services 24/7

5. Borderless access to government information

6. The use of common standards by all government entities

7. The development of appropriate infrastructure for the implementation of e-governance

8. Assuring efficiency of the public sector

9. Securing competitiveness of the national economy

10. And above all, the improvement of services delivered to citizens and businesses in terms of quality, quantity, cost and access

Nevertheless, small states face considerable challenges and obstacles they must overcome if they are to embrace e-governance holistically – not least of which are: costs of technology; lack of infrastructure; limited human capital; and a weak private sector. These constraints will inhibit the design, scope and extent of the strategy. Should the strategy focus on ad hoc projects targeting the resolution of a particular issue or issues in the country, or should it embark upon a holistic approach? To what extent will the design of the strategy be restricted by accessibility to finance? Are smaller projects more likely to be implemented, due to the strong possibility of securing donor assistance, than a holistic e-governance approach?

Small, ad hoc and stand-alone e-governance initiatives are the norm in least developed countries, which often lack a well thought out e-strategy within their national development plans. However, this is not the right approach. An e-governance strategy requires a consistent and interoperable approach if it is to be successful. Ad hoc initiatives will prove far more costly to retrofit for interoperability – and if interoperability cannot be attained, e-governance will not be achieved.

Can the challenges that small states face in achieving e-governance be overcome? A well-designed e-governance strategy that interlinks with human and economic development can act as a powerful catalyst that will secure, over time, the attainment of e-governance.

E-governance framework
A well-designed e-governance strategy should be based on a comprehensive framework. An e-governance framework is introduced here to highlight a complete range of components for a coherent e-governance strategy (see Figure 1.1).

- **The e-governance strategy** is a component of the national ICT strategy. While the national ICT strategy may focus on wide goals of developing and improving ICT infrastructure, encouraging industry growth and economic development and enhancing ICT education, an e-governance strategy focuses on the use of ICTs in government to enable the delivery of **more efficient public services**, allow greater public access to information, make government more **accountable to citizens** and **increase citizen participation** in government decision-making processes. ICTs can be used by governments for public service delivery – from speeding up transactions by providing them online or via mobile devices, to enabling monitoring and feedback of service delivery, which can lead to increases in efficiency and responsiveness. Not only can public trust in government be enhanced, but inclusion and empowerment of groups often excluded from the policy process can be increased through extension of information access and capability to all citizens. Governments can, and should, draw upon the ability of ICTs to facilitate the provision of prompt and **transparent** information online. Transparency portals developed by governments around the world provide free and open access to government information and spending, thus promoting public accountability, decreasing corruption and developing a sense of citizen ownership over government spending priorities (Fung et al. 2010). Transparency is linked to increased accountability, where improvements in the ability to measure government performance through transparency and in the awareness of citizens and civil society through ICTs and the media can enable both vertical and horizontal accountability of government. E-governance programmes describe and project a distinct conceptualisation of the citizen – not only as a customer or consumer, but also as a participant. Citizen-centricity is essential in the delivery of public services, in increasing access to the governing process and in promoting citizen-led government accountability.

Figure 1.1 E-governance framework

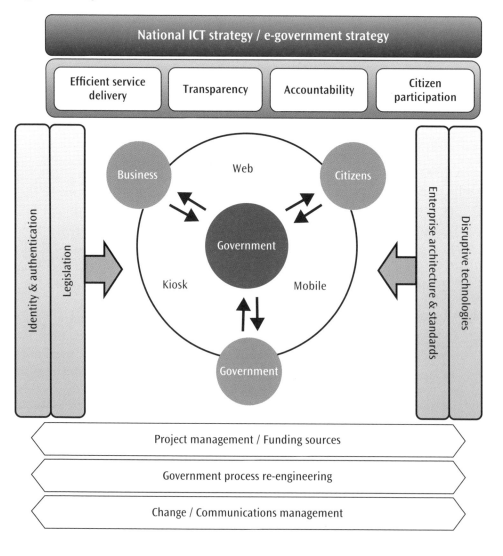

- E-governance is about government using ICTs such as **the internet, mobile devices and kiosks or telecentres** to transform relations with **citizens, the private sector and other government agencies**. However, a specific **citizen identity and authentication** process is important for all secure financial and non-financial transactions of e-governance. Similarly, specific **ICT legislation and technical enterprise architecture** are essential if government is to effectively use ICTs and ensure the legal validity of e-services, the safety of personal and government data, the equal access of electronic services to citizens and the optimal performance of information systems.

- New **disruptive technologies,** including cloud computing, mobile technologies and Web 2.0 offer solutions to many cost- and accessibility-related issues.

- Key to the process of rolling out and sustaining e-governance are good **project management, change and communications management** and **process re-engineering**.

E-governance can only be successfully delivered if citizens have access to the technology, can afford the technology and are able to use the technology. A state-of-the-art e-governance framework will fail unless such fundamentals are in place.

1.5.3 Stages of e-governance

The field of ICT is dominated by normative rather than factual models showing the different stages of e-government evolution. In 2001, Ronaghan offered a model that was part of an international e-government benchmarking effort undertaken by the United Nations and the American Society for Public Administration (Figure 1.2). The model explains five different stages on the path of e-government.

Figure 1.2 Ronaghan's model of the stages of e-government

Emerging	An official government online presence is established.
Enhanced	Government sites increase; information becomes more dynamic.
Interactive	Users can download forms, email officials and interact through the web.
Transactional	Users can actually pay for services and other transactions online.
Seamless	Full integration of e-services across administrative boundaries.

Source: Ronaghan 2001: 2

Ronaghan's model explains that the first stage is just 'a cursory presence on the web'. In this initial stage, a country, state or local government has an official presence on the internet through a limited number of individual governmental pages (mostly developed by single governmental agencies). Governments at this stage usually provide static information about their agencies and some of the public services they offer.

This presence gains more substance during the second stage, where there is 'an enhanced presence in which governmental information is made available on an official website 24/7', and this information is regularly updated. At this stage, a government's official site sometimes serves as an entry point with links to pages of other branches of government, ministries, secretariats, departments and subnational administrative bodies. Some governments also start using electronic mail or search engines at this stage to interact with citizens, businesses and other stakeholders.

The third and fourth stages are interactive and transactional respectively, where people are provided with the means to contribute to government processes by 'interacting' with governmental organisations and officials online and by carrying out 'transactions' on government websites.

During the 'interactive' stage, governments provide access to services in various agencies through a state-wide or national portal. The interaction between citizens and different government agencies increases in this stage, and citizens and businesses can access information according to their different interests. In some cases, passwords are used to access more customised and secure services.

During the 'transactional' stage, citizens and businesses can personalise or customise a national or state-wide portal, which becomes a unique showcase of all the governmental services available in the relevant area of interest. The design of and access to this portal are based according to the needs of different constituencies, while government structures and functions are only secondary criteria. Secure electronic payments can be made through this portal, which facilitates transactions such as tax, fines and services payments.

By the final stage of e-government, there is a seamless horizontal and vertical integration of governmental information and services and the whole of the government system is digitised. Therefore, starting from a basic web presence, e-government initiatives move on to transform into sophisticated mechanisms where all aspects of government information and services are available online and enable all government functions to be carried out on the web. Furthermore, there is inter-departmental and intra-governmental integration of similar services provided by different levels of government. This integration can be virtual, physical or both. At this stage, a reformation of government structures and/or processes begins so that a comprehensive and fundamental vision of the government as a whole can be developed.

It is also relevant to note that the sophistication of the ICTs applied increases at each stage of the e-governance maturity level until the public service system becomes fully integrated and pro-active (Figure 1.3). The model also reflects how businesses and citizens can interact with public authorities (Capgemini et al. 2009). At the initial stage where only basic information is available, the level of maturity is at 20 per cent, graduating to 40 per cent, 60 per cent, 80 per cent and 100 per cent in the consecutive stages. It is the fifth stage where e-governance services reach their maximum level of maturity and sophistication and government services are fully integrated. At this stage, governments take on institutional and administrative reforms that fully utilise the potential of ICTs. The aim is to ensure increased transparency, accountability, efficient service delivery and enhanced citizen participation.

1.6 Conclusion

While debate on the role of ICTs in governance has been growing over the last decade, there is also a general emerging consensus that e-governance is not just about ICTs. It is more holistic in approach and although ICTs are the fundamental enabling factors of any e-governance intervention, many non-ICT factors are equally important prerequisites. These include political will, citizen participation, partnerships and financial sustainability. There are three key strategic guidelines for a successful journey of e-governance. First, to establish governance structures before implementing e-governance: institutes, processes and laws to ensure efficient governance should be

Figure 1.3 The benchmark's five-stage maturity model

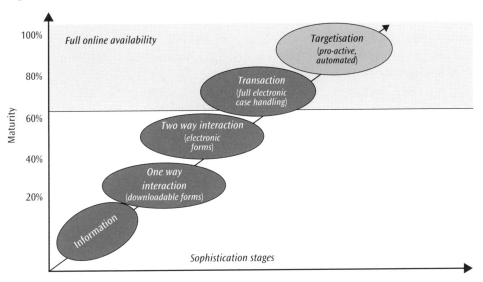

Source: Capgemini et al., 2009: 20

in place before developing any ICT-based interventions. Second, ICT should always be used as an enabler and means, instead of an outcome or end for efficient governance. Third, each e-governance intervention should be based on linking ICTs with the basic pillars of governance such as transparency, accountability, public service delivery and citizen's participation.

References

Abramson, MA, and GE Means (Eds.) (2001), *E-government 2001*, Rowman and Littlefield, Lanham, MD.

Andersen, KV, and HZ Henriksen (2006), 'E-government maturity models: extension of the Layne and Lee model', *Government Information Quarterly*, Vol. 23, 236–248.

Capgemini, R, Europe, IDC, Sogeti and DTI (2009), 'Smarter, Faster, Better eGovernment', 8th Benchmark Measurement, European Commission Directorate General for Information Society and Media, available at: www.dipsanet.es/cipsa/docs/2009-egov_benchmark.pdf (accessed 22 March 2013).

Ciborra, C (2005), 'Interpreting e-Government and Development Efficiency, Transparency or Governance at a distance?', *Information Technology and People*, Vol. 18 No.3, 260–279.

Coursey, D, and D Norris (2008), 'Models of E-Government: Are They Correct? An Empirical Assessment', *Public Administration Review*, Vol. 68 No. 3, 523–36.

Crede, A, and R Mansell (1998), 'Knowledge Societies in a Nutshell – Information Technology for Sustainable Development', International Development Research Centre (IDRC), Ottawa.

Dada, D (2006), 'The Failure of E-Government in Developing Countries: A Literature Review', available at: www.ejisdc.org/ojs2/index.php/ejisdc/article/viewFile/277/176 (accessed 20 August 2010).

Daraja (2011), Monitoring Report 2011: Daraja – Raising the Water Pressure, Twawaza, available at: http://twaweza.org/uploads/files/Daraja%20Monitoring%20Report%202011.pdf (accessed 22 March 2013).

Fraga, E (2002), 'Trends in e-Government: How to Plan, Design, Secure and Measure e-Government', Government Management Information Sciences (GMIS) Conference, Santa Fe, New Mexico, 16–19 June 2002.

Fung, A, H Russon Gilman and J Shkabatur (2010), 'Technology for transparency: Impact case studies from middle income and developing countries', Transparency and Accountability Initiative, available at: www.transparency-initiative.org/wp-content/uploads/2011/05/impact_case_studies_final1.pdf (accessed 22 March 2013).

Gaventa, J, and G Barrett (2010), *So What Difference Does it Make? Mapping the Outcomes of Citizen Engagement*, Institute of Development Studies (IDS), Brighton.

Gubbins, M (2004), 'Global IT spending by sector', *Computing*, 8 April 2004, 28.

Hanna, N (2012), *Open Development: ICT for Governance in Africa*, Africa Public Sector Governance, ICT Unit, World Bank, Washington, DC.

Heacock, R (2010), *'Budget Tracking Tool' Technology for Transformation Network*, available at: http://transparency.globalvoicesonline.org/project/budget-tracking-tool (accessed 22 March 2013).

Heeks, RB (2002), 'Failure, Success and Improvisation of Information Systems Projects in Developing Countries', Development Informatics Working Paper No. 11, University of Manchester, UK.

Heeks, RB (2006), 'Implementing & Managing e-Government', Sage Publications, London.

Institute of Development Studies (IDS) (2010), *An Upside-down View of Governance*, Institute of Development Studies, Brighton.

International Telecommunication Union (ITU) (2008), *Electronic Government for Developing Countries*, International Telecommunication Union, ICT Applications and Cybersecurity Division, ITU: Geneva

ITU (2011), *National e-Strategies for Development Global Status and Perspectives 2010*, ITU, Geneva

Kuriyan, R, S Bailur, BS Gigler, and KR Park (2011), *Technologies for Transparency and Accountability: Implications for ICT Policy and Implementation*, Open Development Technology Alliance and World Bank Publications, Washington, DC.

McGee, R, and J Gaventa (2010), 'Review of the Impact and Effectiveness of Transparency and Accountability Initiatives: Synthesis Report', Transparency and Accountability Initiative Workshop, 14–15 October 2010, Institute of Development Studies, Brighton.

Murillo, M (2012), 'Including all audiences in the government loop: From transparency to empowerment through open government data', W3 Conference, 20 June 2012. Using Open Data: policy modelling, citizen empowerment, data journalism.

National Institute for Smart Government (NISG) (2012), *e-Governance Project Lifecycle: Reading Supplement Handbook*, National e-Governance Plan and Specialised Training for e-Governance Programme, India, available at: http://deity.gov.in/sites/upload_files/dit/files/e-Governance_Project_Lifecycle_Participant_Handbook-5Day_CourseV1_20412.pdf (accessed 22 March 2013).

Parisopoluous, K, E Tambouris and K Tarabanis (2007), 'Analyzing and Comparing European eGovernment Strategies', World Bank, Washington, DC.

Patel, H and D Jacobson (2008), 'Factors Influencing Citizen Adoption of E-Government: A Review and Critical Assessment', Paper 176, European Conference on Information System (ECIS) 2008 Proceedings, Ireland.

Ronaghan, SA (2001), *Benchmarking E-Government: A Global Perspective*, United Nations Division for Public Economics and Public Administration and American Society for Public Administration, New York, available at: http://unpan1.un.org/intradoc/groups/public/documents/UN/UNPAN021547.pdf (accessed 22 March 2013).

Saxena, KBC (2005), 'Towards Excellence in e-Governance', *International Journal of Public Sector Management*, Vol. 18 No. 6, 498–513.

Sobrinh, JH (2011), 'Brazil's Transparency Portal Freely Delivers Information to Citizens', Open Government Partnership, available at: www.opengovpartnership. org/news/brazil%E2%80%99s-transparency-portal-freely-delivers-information-citizens (accessed 20 March 2013).

Twawesa (2010), 'CU@SCHOOL: Tracking School Attendance in Uganda', Twawesa, available at: http://twaweza.org/go/cu-school-tracking-school-attendance-in-uganda (accessed 19 March 2013).

UN Development Programme (UNDP) (2005), 'E-Governance', draft, v. 99, available at: http://sdnhq.undp.org/~raul/egov/pn/egov-pn-v.99.pdf (accessed 20 August 2013).

UN Educational, Scientific and Cultural Organization (UNESCO) (2005), *E-Government Toolkit for Developing Countries*, UNESCO and National Informatics Centre (NIC).

UNESCO (2007), E-Governance Capacity Building, UNESCO WebWorld, available at: http://portal.unesco.org/ci/en/ev.php-URL_ID=2179&URL_DO=DO_TOPIC&URL_SECTION=201.html (accessed 18 March 2013).

UN Parliamentary Assembly (UNPA) and American Society of Public Administration (ASPA) (2001), *Benchmarking e-Government: A Global Perspective*, available at: http://unpan1.un.org/intradoc/groups/public/documents/un/unpan003984. pdf (accessed 22 March 2013).

Vaezi, SK, and HSI Bimar (2009), 'Comparison of E-readiness assessment models', Scientific Research and Essay, May 2009, Vol. 4 No. 5, 501–512.

World Bank (1994), *The World Bank and Participation*, Operations Policy Department, World Bank, Washington, DC.

World Bank (2001), 'Issue Note: E-Government and the World Bank'. November 5, World Bank, Washington, DC.

World Bank (2004), 'World Development Report-2004- Making Services Work for Poor', World Bank, Washington, DC.

World Bank (2012), 'Information and Communication Technology for Governance (ICT4GOV) Program', World Bank Institute Capacity Development and Results, Washington, DC.

Chapter 2

e-Governance in Small States

Omer Awan

Thirty-two of the Commonwealth's fifty-four members are classified as small states (see Table 2.1). These are generally defined as countries with populations of less than 1.5 million, but which also have several shared characteristics – including susceptibility to natural disasters, environmental change and income volatility. Geographical isolation and the openness of their economies are also important issues for small states.

Of the 32 small states in the Commonwealth, 25 are classified as small island states. Cyprus and Malta are small island states, albeit not 'small island developing states' (SIDS). The Commonwealth's small states also include developing countries such as Botswana, The Gambia, Jamaica, Lesotho, Namibia and Papua New Guinea, which although they have populations of more than 1.5 million, share the characteristics of 'small states'.

Table 2.1 Small states of the Commonwealth

Africa	*Asia*	*Caribbean*	*Pacific*	*Europe*
Botswana	Maldives	Antigua and Barbuda	Kiribati	Cyprus
Lesotho	Brunei Darussalam	Barbados	Fiji	Malta
Mauritius		The Bahamas	Nauru	
Namibia		Belize	Papua New Guinea	
Seychelles		Dominica	Samoa	
Swaziland		Grenada	Solomon Islands	
The Gambia		Guyana	Tonga	
		Jamaica	Tuvalu	
		St Kitts and Nevis	Vanuatu	
		St Lucia		
		St Vincent and the Grenadines		
		Trinidad and Tobago		

2.1 Why e-governance in small states?

According to the latest UN *E-Government Survey* (UN 2012), which included 190 countries, more than half of Commonwealth small member countries (17 of 32 states) are ranked in bottom half of the rankings in terms of their online government services. None of these small states rank in the top 20 countries, with only 4 of them in the top 50 countries; Malta ranks top of the Commonwealth small states, at 35. The figures arc alarming considering the evolution of ICTs and their effectiveness in the area of governance and service delivery. They clearly show that the access and use of ICTs for governance are at a formative stage in these countries, with millions of people still outside the inclusive net of benefits.

Table 2.2 E-government rankings of Commonwealth small states

Commonwealth small states	E-government index 2012	E-government ranking 2012	E-government ranking 2010
Malta	0.7131	35	30
Barbados	0.6566	44	40
Cyprus	0.6508	45	42
Antigua and Barbuda	0.6345	49	55
Brunei Darussalam	0.6250	54	68
Bahamas, The	0.5793	65	65
Trinidad and Tobago	0.5731	67	67
Dominica	0.5561	73	105
Grenada	0.5479	75	99
St Kitts and Nevis	0.5272	81	75
Seychelles	0.5192	84	104
St Vincent and the Grenadines	0.5177	85	94
St Lucia	0.5122	90	88
Mauritius	0.5066	93	77
Maldives	0.4994	95	92
Fiji	0.4672	105	113
Jamaica	0.4552	108	89
Guyana	0.4549	109	106
Tonga	0.4405	111	116

(Continued)

Table 2.2 E-government rankings of Commonwealth small states (cont.)

Commonwealth small states	E-government index 2012	E-government ranking 2012	E-government ranking 2010
Samoa	0.4358	114	115
Namibia	0.3937	123	125
Botswana	0.4186	121	117
Belize	0.3923	124	120
Tuvalu	0.3539	134	N/A
Vanuatu	0.3512	135	155
Lesotho	0.3501	136	121
Nauru	0.3242	141	N/A
Swaziland	0.3179	144	145
Kiribati	0.2998	149	N/A
Gambia, The	0.2688	161	167
Solomon Islands	0.2416	168	156
Papua New Guinea	0.2147	177	171

Source: UN E-Government Survey 2012

While each Commonwealth small state is unique – which requires their development programmes to be planned and executed according to their specific historical, cultural and social context – understanding the characteristics and development problems shared by such states can improve e-governance planning and support.

These particular characteristics and development challenges also mean that such states in particular can benefit from e-governance initiatives, as these can play a crucial role in enhancing the ability of the public sector to overcome such barriers.

2.1.1 Isolation

Isolation marks most small developing states, whether they are islands, landlocked or located far from major markets. The issue of isolation creates adverse effects for small developing states in two ways:

- First, this distance makes their transport costs high and prevents them from turning to major markets to compensate for the drawbacks of their small and limited capacity local markets (Commonwealth Secretariat and World Bank

Joint Task Force 2000). These natural limitations also create hindrances for businesses and investors, who can be discouraged from entering these isolated markets by the geographical and physical barriers to access for information and government processes.

- Second, isolation of communities within the small developing states limits the flow of information, and inadequate communication channels caused by isolation negatively impact bargaining capabilities. This makes local economies more vulnerable and also restricts citizen participation in government processes (Favaro 2008).

This then makes ICTs and their virtual presence even more valuable for small developing states. For example, a government's online presence becomes much more fundamental if a state is to overcome these barriers. In the era of globalisation where e-commerce and e-trade have become an unavoidable phenomenon, small developing states cannot survive without leveraging the power of the digital economy. The online presence of a government's institutes, ministries, processes and information – for example, in the areas of tourism and investment – would definitely assist small developing states to achieve a competitive advantage in global markets by overcoming the geographical and physical barriers caused by isolation.

ICTs are also an important mechanism to enhance the ability of the public sector to cost-effectively and efficiently reach and tailor services to isolated communities within the state, to include them in public decision-making and to network government. To achieve cost-effective, relevant and personalised services, e-governance needs to be client-centric; moreover, customer focus and addressing clients' changing needs enhances democratic dialogue (CceGov 2007).

2.1.2 Susceptibility to natural disasters and income volatility

Environmental disasters and income volatility are two much interlinked features of small developing states, which affect their endeavours for sustainable economic development.

Disasters, both natural and as a result of human activity, are on the rise, with grave consequences for the survival and livelihood of individuals. This is particularly the case for those living in small island states, where disasters can quickly reverse hard-won economic gains. The impacts of disasters have been estimated at 10–15 per cent of their gross domestic product (GDP) (Commonwealth Secretariat 2009). Small island states, in particular due to their locations, are often vulnerable to environmental hazards such as cyclones, hurricanes, volcanic eruptions, earthquakes, drought and environmental change, which affect the entire population and economy.

It has become more imperative for developing small states to adopt ICT-enabled e-governance initiatives to tackle natural disasters. Effective e-governance services incorporate the whole range of ICTs to provide support to citizens at all stages of disaster risk reduction (DRR). ICTs are not only important for the development of efficient environmental early-warning systems, but also assist citizens during a response to a natural disaster. Government-owned internet/SMS-based services can provide real-time information and solutions to citizens. For instance, in response to Haiti's earthquake in 2010, open-source crisis-mapping software was applied to collect masses of real-time information coming through ICTs and social media regarding immediate needs. An international group of self-organised volunteers updated the information and made it publicly available online to assist recovery efforts (Kelman 2012).

There is also often a higher incidence of poverty, more uneven income distribution and higher income volatility in small states when compared to large states. The reason behind income volatility, besides environmental disasters, is the high level of exports/ imports and low variation in production and trade, due to the small domestic market and resource base. This leaves these countries exposed to changes in world markets and more vulnerable to external economic shocks. Where one prevailing activity has declined, it has tended to be replaced with another, increasing the vulnerability of the population to changes in the external environment (Commonwealth Secretariat and World Bank Joint Task Force 2000).

Income volatility and environmental hazards necessitate the need for external economic relations (i.e. access to global capital markets), but these very factors are the reasons why private markets see small states as more risky than larger states – so that market access becomes more difficult for these states. It also play a crucial role in improving overall economic performance, through magnifying access and use of fundamental development resources. Moreover, e-governance policies that support the growth of the ICT sector, the creation of jobs and an increase in viable business possibilities, as well as supporting the infrastructure, access and use of ICTs to strengthen commercial, health, educational, cultural and public services, can help states to withstand external shocks.

2.1.3 Limited institutional capacity

Higher input costs and the absence of economies of scale in the provision of public goods and services explain why small states tend to have larger governments (Alesina and Wacziarg 1998). There are fixed costs in creating public institutions and providing public services such as policing, education, justice, social services and foreign affairs. Since these public services must be provided regardless of population size, the cost is higher per person (or per taxpayer) in small states. E-governance therefore becomes a vital intervention to achieve economies of scale in the long run. ICT solutions such as cloud computing – remotely hosted IT infrastructure and applications – mobile devices and networking can lead to significant cost-savings for small state governments (Cas and Ota 2008).

Moreover, small states have limited public and private capacity. In the private sector this results in restricted development, while in the public sector it leads to small states being unable to compete and participate in the global political arena. This negatively impacts e-government infrastructure development on the one hand, and the securing of local and international funds for e-governance initiatives on the other. E-government initiatives, such as national ICT strategies, must therefore be developed according to the specific country context, resources and needs. Technologies such as mobile devices and kiosks offer cheap, simple and convenient solutions to deliver e-government services, particularly in low-resource, low-capacity conditions.

2.1.4 Importance of improved governance for small states

The strategic outcomes of e-governance, including participatory government, transparency and accountability, help small states to achieve better governance. Since small states are more vulnerable to high public and external debt, the quality of their institutions matters even more than in large countries (Bräutigam and Woolcock 2001). Small states with high-quality institutions have less growth volatility, and are more likely to benefit from higher rates of economic growth (ibid). It has been claimed that for lower-income small states in particular, improving governance and the quality of institutions raises the public debt threshold (i.e. the public debt that countries can safely sustain without experiencing debt crisis). There is also evidence that better institutional quality is associated in emerging markets with prudent borrowing and a more countercyclical fiscal policy response (IMF 2003).

Furthermore, good governance, including increased transparency, can support citizen participation, help investors make better-informed assessments and can reassure markets and donors on the government's fiscal goals. Enhanced transparency is particularly important for small states, because they are at an informational disadvantage compared to large countries – foreign investors tend to know less about them – while at the same time they are more open and dependent on foreign capital. In an increasingly globalised world, small states need to compete with large countries that investors are more familiar with, that benefit from economies of scale and that suffer less from isolation.

2.2 E-governance prerequisites for small states

Keeping in view the unique issues, attributes and importance of e-governance for Commonwealth small states, it is important to note that e-governance is not a 'stand-alone' and 'ready to implement' process. In 2008 the Commonwealth Telecommunications Organisation (CTO) conducted a survey that demonstrated the bleak picture of how e-governance initiatives have fared in developing/transitional countries, evaluating 35 per cent of the initiatives as total failures, 50 per cent as partial failures and only 15 per cent as successes (CTO 2008). This leads to the question of what influences or causes the failure of the majority of initiatives. The report suggests that a number of critical factors that result in the failure of e-government projects include unrealistic project goals, inaccurate assessments of resources, poor reporting of the project's status, unmanaged risks, poor communication among stakeholders and poor project management.

The framework proposed in this handbook aims to offer a set of guidelines for e-governance strategists, to help them better plan and implement projects by analysing and evaluating the opportunities and threats in their external environment and by settling on a set of prerequisites necessary to maximise the chances of project success.

The introduction of e-governance in small states requires a set of guidelines that cater to the specific needs of these countries. The following 'SWIFT Framework' intends to do just that (Figure 2.1).

2.2.1. Situational analysis and standardisation
E-governance is about providing more citizen-centred services, these being services that are attuned to the needs and circumstances of the people or the situational context. Factors here include cultural and linguistic suitability, as culture is the aggregate of

Figure 2.1 Prerequisite conditions (SWIFT) analysis for the development of e-governance

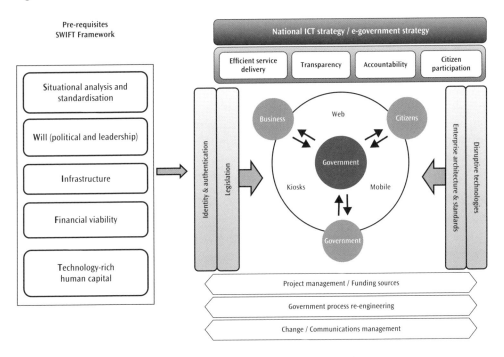

individual personality traits that, along with historical background, shapes the values shared by members of a society (Ali et al. 2009). Such factors have a significant influence on ICT adoption and therefore on the readiness of a region for e-government initiatives (Maitland and Bauer 2001).

Hence the digital divide is not only caused by income disparity, but is also associated with cultural attitudes towards technology (ibid). If people perceive e-governance initiatives to be worthwhile and easy to use, then they would be much more readily accepted and adopted (Patel and Jacobson 2008). For example, citizens would be more supportive and would be more regular users of a public website to pay their electricity bills if they recognised the benefits it brought them in terms of saving time and effort going to a government office.

Another important aspect of citizens' attitudes towards e-government are the risks they perceive to be associated with it – such as increased taxation if e-government projects are too expensive, or loss of local employment of non-IT experts whose jobs may be compromised due to the introduction of e-services (Sjoberg and Schreiner 2005). Such perceptions of risk may propel people to resist change, sometimes even when they recognise the benefits that may accompany the change. Therefore, unless context-appropriate e-government initiatives are introduced at a suitable pace and with understanding of the local context, they cannot be expected to go very far. Creating an ICT-receptive environment and inducing positive perceptions of e-government initiatives among the local population, through advertising their advantages and benefits, is an important strategy to ensure their success.

The goal of standardisation is to design e-government projects so that they are well co-ordinated, uniform and so easy to implement and utilise. First, it is general business knowledge that a well-planned strategy with clear objectives is the backbone of a successful project. According to De' (2006), most e-government programmes fail in developing countries around the world due to a lack of direction and continued support by the responsible government department. Such projects may have been perceived as a way to fulfil the growing demand for 'computerisation', without a clear understanding of the problem being addressed or the adequate design of such systems. Or they may have dealt with only the immediate aspects of these problems, without evaluating their more in-depth causes.

Second, countrywide success of e-government projects requires co-ordination among different government departments responsible for the diverse aspects of e-government programmes, both within an area or city and between them. Without such co-ordination and without a cohesive strategy, the e-government scheme is at greater risk of failure (Ali et al. 2009). Moreover, standardisation of e-government projects enables government to monitor and evaluate them more effectively, without which determining the causes of their success or failure would be next to impossible.

Third, a methodology for the identification and authentication of users of e-government services is important to both safeguard privacy and to ensure that users can be authenticated. Electronic identity authentication can take many forms, such as national identity numbers, social security numbers and 'smart' identity cards. These allow citizens to authenticate themselves in an easy and comprehensively secure way whenever they access e-government applications, and enable the creation of an architecture for secure e-government electronic identity management.

Therefore, for an e-government project to be able to achieve its desired goal of improved service delivery to citizens, it is essential that its objectives and goals are clearly predetermined and that the situational context is understood by officials responsible for conducting such projects. In addition, all aspects of the projects must be co-ordinated and standardised to ensure smooth progress towards the end goal (see Chapter 5 for details on the process of standardisation). E-governance solutions must be adapted, not simply adopted, to ensure that the design of those solutions matches developing country situations (Bishop and Savoury 2004) and that there is not a large gap between the design of the e-government projects and the realities of the state where they are introduced.

2.2.2 Will (political and leadership)

All government reforms require 'political will' to succeed and be sustained, and e-government reforms are no different (PCIP 2002). Political will exists when senior decision-makers have the determination to exercise leadership in the face of resistance and obstacles. Some government officials, particularly in developing countries, are prone to distrust any new initiative that may seem to challenge their prestige. According to Ali et al. (2009), there is the risk that some government officials could view the introduction of ICT into government as a loss of their status and power. Furthermore, the traditional bureaucracy within government may resist changes in procedures and possibly the increased transparency that e-government will provide (PCIP 2002). If e-government initiatives lack support from the people who have to carry them out, then not much can be expected of their outcome (Ali et al. 2009).

It is imperative to realise that all successful e-government projects are backed by a visionary leader or leaders who push for change, even through tough times. The right leader is authoritative, a risk-taker, is willing to secure funds for the programme, will commit time on a continuing basis and will openly endorse and advocate for e-government (PCIP 2002). The leader or leaders of small states must also:

- Ensure that the role of ICT is strategically linked to economic growth and national development of the state.

- Be able to vouch for the benefits of ICT usage from a personal standpoint. The leader must champion the cause for e-government and take ownership of the project, even in the face of opposition from within the public service or ruling political party. The champion should endeavour to build support both within and outside his or her administration.

- Seek support in the private sector from those already convinced of the need for greater technology utilisation.

- Have to depend on consultants, suppliers or other states. Since small states do not possess all the requisite human and financial resources, the involvement of top public servants in the planning phase may help them to appreciate how their units could benefit. Ultimately they might become advocates for the e-government initiative, and so convince others of the need for it (Bishop and Savoury 2004).

- Realise that the best way to resolve resistance is to involve all stakeholders and government officials at all levels in the planning and implementation of the initiatives (this process is further detailed in Chapter 3). This will encourage familiarity with and 'ownership' of projects, which will in turn increase their sustainability and chances of success (PCIP 2002).

2.2.3 Infrastructure

Before analysing the state of ICT infrastructure and access to infrastructure, and before e-governance can be introduced in any country, its advocates need to ensure that there are no laws that prevent putting information and services online. The development of e-government initiatives can be assisted by modifying or removing laws intended for the non-digital world (infoDev 2008). An enabling environment needs to be created which supports e-development and allows ICTs to perform to their optimal level for social and economic progress (Guermazi and Satola 2005).

However, the most important prerequisite in terms of infrastructure is that the realisation of e-government programmes depends greatly on whether people have access to and user-knowledge of the internet. Hence a widely accessible and affordable communications infrastructure, together with a regulatory framework, is one of the essential factors for the successful delivery of government services online. ICT access and e-government must be closely linked. One significant way to do this is by building numerous computerised service centres across the country, as most service users in developing countries and small states do not yet have access to the internet in their homes (Bhatia et al. 2009). The increased availability of e-government services that save citizens and businesses time and money can also raise demand for ICT and boost future infrastructure development.

Table 2.3 shows two clear trends that can assist small states in developing their future e-governance strategies. First, despite immense internet growth over the last decade, many small states lag far behind in terms of access to the internet (the primary source of e-governance applications so far). More than 50 per cent of small states still have fewer than 50 internet users per 100 inhabitants, and so are lacking a major prerequisite for e-governance. Second, an additional delivery channel to increase the reach of government services is via mobile technology, particularly given the ubiquity of mobile phones in small and developing countries. Table 2.3 suggests that mobile subscription growth has reached exponential levels, with more than 10 Commonwealth small states having gone beyond 100 per cent growth rates (see Chapter 6 for more information on m-government).

Furthermore, a lack of ICT infrastructure within government departments at the central and state levels also poses a barrier to e-governance implementation. States that have mostly paper-based systems face two main obstacles: first, automating internal records and processes, and second, making information and services publicly available online. However, these obstacles can also be looked upon as opportunities to redesign inadequate processes before they are computerised (infoDev 2008) (see Chapter 4 for information on government process re-engineering). Therefore, such countries would benefit from adopting e-government-specific legislation and building a strong communications infrastructure, as the initial steps towards countrywide implementation. New laws addressing all aspects of e-government can be made at one time before starting projects; alternatively, incremental changes in the laws and procedures can be taken with each progressive step of the process (ibid.) (see Chapter 5 for details on legislation).

Table 2.3 Access to ICTs in Commonwealth small states

Commonwealth small states	Mobile/cellular subscriptions per 100	Number of internet users per 100
Antigua and Barbuda	182	82
Bahamas, The	86	65
Barbados	127	72
Belize	64	N/A (12.7 in 2010)
Botswana	143	7
Brunei Darussalam	109	56
Cyprus	98	58
Dominica	164	51
Fiji	84	28
Gambia, The	N/A (85 in 2010)	11
Grenada	N/A (117 in 2010)	N/A (33 in 2010)
Guyana	69	32
Jamaica	108	32

(Continued)

Table 2.3 Access to ICTs in Commonwealth small states (cont.)

Commonwealth small states	Mobile/cellular subscriptions per 100	Number of internet users per 100
Kiribati	14	10
Lesotho	48	4
Maldives	166	34
Malta	125	69
Mauritius	99	35
Namibia	0.3937	12
Nauru	N/A	N/A
Papua New Guinea	34	2
St Kitts and Nevis	N/A (153 in 2010)	N/A (76 in 2010)
St Lucia	123	42
St Vincent and the Grenadines	121	43
Samoa	N/A (91 in 2010)	N/A (7 in 2010)
Seychelles	146	44
Solomon Islands	50	6
Swaziland	64	20
Trinidad and Tobago	136	55
Tonga	53	25
Tuvalu	22	30
Vanuatu	N/A (119 in 2010	N/A (8 in 2010)

Source: World Bank 2013

While building new telecommunications infrastructure, it is important to keep in mind the vulnerability of small states to environmental disasters. Their geographical location often makes them susceptible to natural disasters such as hurricanes, cyclones, volcanic eruptions, earthquakes, landslides and floods brought about by a rise in sea levels. These natural phenomena can severely disturb the performance of the economy and cause a significant amount of damage to the physical environment, as was apparent by the 2004 tsunami in the Indian Ocean (Downes 2005). While keeping the constraints of new emerging technologies like 'cloud computing' in mind, this can still be a suitable solution for the small development states (see Chapter 6 for details).

2.2.4 Financial viability

Income inequality within and between nations has headed the agenda of development organisations for many decades, and has apparently continued into the digital world. Here the digital divide between nations remains extensive: a person in a high-income country is more than 22 times more likely to be an internet user than one in a low-income country, although there are signs that ICT diffusion is slowly becoming more equal (UNCTAD 2006). This digital divide not only exists between countries and regions, but also within a country's borders, most commonly between rich and poor, between men and women, and between urban and rural areas (ibid).

Financial constraints are a major factor in the digital divide; they prevent the less privileged from owning personal computers and being able to pay the price of expensive broadband services and internet access (Ali et al. 2009). Moreover, urban areas receive an excessively large part of public and private ICT investment in relation to the rest of the country, and usually have at least a basic communications infrastructure. They are therefore able to take better advantage of ICTs compared to rural areas, where there are lower incentives for ICT service providers to invest.

On another note, a lack of funding from the government can serve as a major impediment on the path to e-governance success. Most developing country governments have small budgets and many priorities, and there is more competition for the distribution of public funds between different sectors. Thus, e-governance initiatives need to demonstrate that they would benefit a large number of people in order to justify their costs. One way of doing this is to boost usage, by promoting initiatives through multiple traditional media channels (PCIP 2002).

Before initiating e-governance projects, a government must have sufficient funds for long-term viability and sustainability, as well as a group of ICT-educated or trained officials to manage and conduct the projects (see Chapter 3 for more details). Additionally, it must be acknowledged from the outset that all the benefits of a countrywide project can never fully be reaped until it is made accessible for every single citizen, thus combatting the problem of the digital divide arising out of disparity of income distribution. E-governance and increased investment in ICT infrastructure is also in itself a strategy for income generation.

Commonwealth small states are often highly dependent on external economic relations for survival – from dependence on migrant labour remittances to maintain living standards, to overseas development assistance to supplement domestic financial resources (Downes 2005). However, the available data for the Caribbean indicates that there was a general reduction in overseas development assistance (ODA) as a percentage of gross national income over the decade 1995–2004. Recent efforts have been made by developed countries to assist developing countries to ease their debt problem through the writing off and rescheduling of accumulated debts (ibid).

Given the financial constraints, it is essential for small developing states to form and maintain alliances to receive financial assistance and save costs for ICT projects. There can be many such alliances. However, developing small states may wish to consider the following options:

- **Alliances within government** – and between different government departments – in order to receive financial assistance for ICT projects.

- **Alliances between government and citizens/non-governmental organisations (NGOs).**

- **Alliances between government and the private sector** – such as outsourcing of projects, when this is deemed to be in the best interests of all. Governments can also learn from the application of ICTs in commercial organisations.

- **Alliances between governments** – some developed countries may provide assistance in designing, implementing and funding ICT projects, but these must not become 'donor-led'. Similarly, networking with governments in other developed countries which have undertaken similar projects should reduce the prospect of 'reinventing the wheel'. A government's procurement process can also benefit from alliances with external entities, e.g. suppliers and trading partners (Bishop and Savoury 2004).

New technologies that are usually developed in larger and more advanced countries have been slowly reaching small states, mainly for personal consumption purposes (and for limited use for production purposes). Nevertheless, the goal of developing a partnership for development still needs to be actively pursued. Small states still face major challenges, which require technical and financial resources from the developed world (Downes 2005).

2.2.5 Technology-rich human capital

Being ICT literate is a prerequisite for government officials responsible for conducting e-governance projects, and for citizens to be able to utilise them to their full potential (ibid). This is possible when ICT education is prevalent in the concerned country (see Chapter 3 for strategies to build ICT human capacity). Small states generally have a fairly good level of primary education; however, the migration of skilled personnel to more developed countries leads to a shortage of well-trained teachers. According to Downes (2005) teachers, along with nurses, are the most significant migrant group of persons from several developing countries in recent years. While a good-quality primary school education level is crucial to the development of the human resource base of a country, the development of universal secondary level education is seen as vital to meeting labour market needs. Small states have a long way to go in this area, as few countries have achieved universal secondary level education.

This then raises the question of the presence of an ICT-skilled labour force for the implementation of ICT projects. A large number of skilled people migrate from small states to developed countries in search of work and cultural experiences, which has been propelled through the mass media and tourism. Criminal activities such as the drugs trade, money laundering and piracy have arisen in small states, influenced by a decline in traditional areas of economic activity; these also have a significant impact on societal values and the nature of economic production. Moreover, feelings of political exclusion and powerlessness on the part of citizens in small states also impacts upon the movement of skilled labour forces (Downes 2005).

Although remittances from migration have been valuable to small countries, the cultural foundation of these countries has been changed significantly. In addition, the loss of skilled human resources adversely affects the provision of high-quality services in some of these small countries (for example, health and education). What is more, the limited financial and human resources associated with small states restricts their ability to manage the development process in an efficient and effective manner. Small states usually provide the same range of public services as large states, but have a much lower capacity to manage the administrative systems (ibid).

2.3 Conclusion

While each small state has unique characteristics, small states share some common developmental and public services challenges due to their geographical attributes, making a strong case for e-governance to convert these challenges into opportunities. However, while there is great potential for e-government initiatives to help small states overcome challenges in good governance, transparency, citizen participation and economic development, it is important to understand, analyse and evaluate the opportunities and threats in the external environment before designing and implementing e-governance programmes. Neglecting to analyse these factors may result in waste of valuable resources, delaying the benefits of e-governance and missing the desired targets of any e-governance interventions.

The SWIFT Framework aims to assist decision-makers from small states in determining the status of the five key prerequisites for the development of successful e-government initiatives, and therefore identify priority areas for further action.

References

Alesina, A and Wacziarg, R (1998), 'Openness, Country Size and Government,' *Journal of Public Economics*, Vol. 69, 305–21.

Ali, M, V Weerakkody and R El-Haddadeh (2009), 'The Impact of National Culture on E-Government Implementation: A Comparison Case Study', *Proceedings of the Fifteenth Americas Conference on Information Systems*, San Francisco, California 6–9

August 2009, available at: http://bura.brunel.ac.uk/bitstream/2438/3660/1/Culture%20and%20eGov_Final.pdf (accessed 20 August 2010).

Bhatia, D, SC Bhatnagar and J Tominaga (2009), 'How Do Manual and E-Government Services Compare? Experiences from India', ICT Regulation Toolkit, available at: www.ictregulationtoolkit.org/en/Publication.3820.html (accessed on 8 March 2013).

Bishop, S and S Savoury (2004), *Towards E-Government in a Small State: An AGILE Framework*, Idea Group Publishing, USA.

Bräutigam, D, and M Woolcock (2001), 'The Role of Institutions in Managing Vulnerability and Opportunity in Small Developing Countries. Small States in a Global Economy,' Discussion Paper No. 2001/07, United Nations University/WIDER, Helsinki.

Cas, SM, and R Ota (2008), *Big Government, High Debt, and Fiscal Adjustment in Small States*, International Monetary Fund (IMF), Washington, DC.

CceGov (2007), Citizen-centric eGovernment study, available at: www.ccegov.eu (accessed on 8 March 2013).

Commonwealth Secretariat (2009), 'Commonwealth Secretariat's Statement to the 2nd Global Platform on Disaster Risk Reduction', 16–19 June 2009, Geneva, Switzerland.

Commonwealth Secretariat and World Bank Joint Task Force (2000), *Small States – Meeting Challenges in the Global Economy*, Report of the Commonwealth Secretariat/World Bank Joint Task Force on Small States), London.

Commonwealth Telecommunications Organisation (CTO) (2008), 'E-Government For Development Information Exchange', University of Manchester, available at: www.egov4dev.org/success/sfrates.shtml (accessed on 8 March 2013).

De', R (2006), 'The Impact of Indian E-Government Initiatives: Issues of Poverty and Vulnerability Reduction, and Conflict', *Regional Development Dialogue*, Vol. 27 No. 2, 88–100.

Downes, A (2005), 'Progress Towards Achieving the Millennium Development Goals in the Small States of the Commonwealth', available at: www.eclac.cl/portofspain/noticias/paginas/6/37516/22_MDG_Report_-_Downes_and_Downes_-_Millenniumm_Dev_Goals.pdf (accessed on 6 March 2013)

Favaro, E (2008), 'Small states, smart solutions: improving connectivity and increasing the effectiveness of public services', World Bank, Washington, DC, available at: http://siteresources.worldbank.org/INTDEBTDEPT/Resources/468980-1206974166266/4833916-1206989877225/SmallStatesComplete.pdf (accessed on 8 March 2013).

Guermazi, B, and D Satola (2005), 'Chapter 2: Creating the "Right" Enabling Environment for ICT', in RSchware (Ed.), *E-Development: From Excitement to Effectiveness*, available at: http://www-wds.worldbank.org/servlet/WDSContentServer/WDSP/IB/2005/11/08/000090341_20051108163202/Rendered/PDF/341470EDevelopment.pdf (accessed on 5 March 2013).

infoDev (2008), 'Chapter 12: Infrastructure and the Digital Divide', infoDev
    e-Government Tool Kit, available at: http://egov.comesa.int/index.php/en/
    e-government-toolkit/57-infodev-e-government-toolkit-contents (accessed on
    8 March 2013).

International Monetary Fund (2003), *World Economic Outlook, September 2003: Public
    Debt in Emerging Markets*, World Economic and Financial Surveys, IMF,
    Washington, DC.

Kelman, I (2012), 'SIDS and ICTs: Applications for Disaster Risk Reduction, Including
    Climate Change Adaptation', Summary Report Panel on ICTs and Small Island
    Developing States at the Fifth International Conference on Information and
    Communication Technologies and Development (ICTD 2012), Atlanta, USA,
    12 March 2012.

Maitland, CF, and JM Bauer (2001), 'National level culture and global diffusion: The
    case of the Internet', in CEss (Ed.), *Culture, technology, communication: Towards an
    intercultural global village*, State University of New York Press, Albany, NY,
    87–128.

Pacific Council on International Policy (PCIP) (2002), *Roadmap for E-government in the
    Developing World: 10 Questions E-Government Leaders Should Ask Themselves*, Pacific
    Council on International Policy, The Working Group on E-Government in the
    Developing World, available at: www.itu.int/wsis/docs/background/themes/
    egov/pacific_council.pdf (accessed on 8 March 2013).

Patel, H, and D Jacobson (2008), 'Factors Influencing Citizen Adoption of
    E-Government: A Review and Critical Assessment', Paper 176, *ECIS 2008
    Proceedings*, London School of Economics, available at: http://is2.lse.ac.uk/asp/
    aspecis/20080090.pdf (accessed 22 August 2010).

Sjoberg, S, and C Schreiner (2005), 'How Do Learners in Different Cultures Relate to
    Science and Technology? Results and Perspectives from the Project ROSE (the
    Relevance of Science Education)', Vol. 6 No. 2, available at: www.ils.uio.no/
    english/rose/network/countries/norway/eng/nor-sjoberg-apfslt2005.pdf
    (accessed on 6 March 2013).

United Nations (2012), 'UN E-government Survey – E-government for People',
    available at: http://unpan1.un.org/intradoc/groups/public/documents/un/
    unpan048065.pdf (accessed on 6 March 2013).

UN Conference on Trade and Development (UNCTAD) (2006), *The Digital Divide
    Report: ICT Diffusion Index, 2005*, available at: www.unctad.org/Templates/
    webflyer.asp?docid=6994&intItemID=2068&lang=1 (accessed on 5 March 2013).

World Bank (2013), World Bank Data, available at: http://data.worldbank.org/
    indicator (accessed on 3 March 2013).

Chapter 3

e-Governance Management – Critical Success Factors

David Spiteri Gingell

Successful e-governance not only depends on the existence of prerequisite conditions, as highlighted in the previous chapter, but also on the ability of the government to implement e-governance and the ability of citizens to adopt and use it. This chapter highlights good practices in terms of leadership, corporate governance, consolation processes, financing, monitoring and evaluation, and ICT capacity building.

3.1 A clear vision

E-governance is traditionally seen as a reinvention of how a government delivers its services, interacts with its citizens and maintains transparency and accountability. This is a definition that fits well with an advanced society, wherein the level of ICT infrastructure is well-developed, legal instruments are in place, trust and confidence in the governing institutions is stable, literacy is high, health institutions are well-established and the digital divide is far less pervasive.

An agreed national vision for e-government is a unifying mechanism to promote development. The national vision:

- minimises the possibility of overlooking important factors in various sectors;

- ensures the maximising of linkages within and between sectors; and

- provides for the unified participation and 'ownership' of the e-government strategy.

3.2 Political leadership

The presence of political leadership to sponsor the strategy and, subsequently, steward its implementation is of paramount importance. While this applies to any major policy design and implementation process, the presence of a powerful political champion for e-government carries greater importance, given that the implementation of e-government transcends different ministries or departments, as well as policy sectors. Moreover, as e-government is a government transformation initiative – not a technology project – it should not be led by technicians, but by policy-makers.

This raises the question of whether political leadership for e-government should be at a central, co-ordinating level or whether it should be decentralised. The experience of Organisation for Economic Co-operation and Development (OECD) countries with e-government shows that decentralised e-government leadership can lead to uncertainty about overall direction if this is not counterbalanced by clear identification of leaders' roles and responsibilities. Unco-ordinated development – with advancement in narrow areas and no progress in remaining areas – restricts broad-based progress and has contributed to the continuing widening of the digital divide within countries (OECD 2005). If elements that are of critical importance to the development of e-government are decentralised to different political responsibility holders, then the approach to e-government will be disjointed at best and fragmented at worst.

Box 3.1   A politically centralised approach to e-government: New Zealand

The minister responsible for the successful delivery of e-government is the minister for state services. The State Services Commission (SSC) was given the following role in the e-government programme:

Strategy: Develop and manage the delivery of an overarching e-government strategy, as well as supporting policies, standards and guidelines

Leadership: Facilitate uptake by government agencies of the e-government vision

Co-ordination/collaboration: Identify opportunities for collaboration across government agencies; leverage existing information management and technology investment, and provide co-ordination for multi-agency e-government projects

Policy: Provide e-government policy advice to the minister of state services

Monitoring: Monitor progress toward achieving the e-government vision

The SSC has a central role in defining and achieving the government's objectives for e-government. The delivery of e-government is the responsibility of all government agencies in partnership with the SSC.

This means that with regard to the technological aspect of the e-government framework, unless policy relating to technology is already centralised, a policy change will be required. Experience shows that a policy towards a centralised ICT framework approach will be resisted, as ministries and agencies will see this both as a brake on the ability to deliver on policy goals, as well as a loss of line authority to the centre. Thus, the identification of a strong minister as the loci of political responsibility for e-government in the first phase of the e-government development journey is believed to be key.

In certain jurisdictions, responsibility for e-government and ICT has been assumed by the prime minister. In other jurisdictions, it has been the minister for finance or the minister responsible for public services/state services. In any event, e-government must be closely identified with the national leadership.

In states where ICT policy, for different reasons, may have been seen as a sector of secondary importance, or where there are highly-skilled human capital gaps, the creation of one organisational entity with a mandate for e-government is appropriate. This may consist of the establishment of an information society and economy or an e-government portfolio, as the case may be, as either a separate portfolio or part of another portfolio – for example, of a telecommunications and information society. This would constitute far more than a symbolic message. It would demonstrate that the government is sincere in its commitment to transform the country into an information society and economy through the implementation of an e-government strategy, as well as – by default of the fact that a ministry is created – that funds will be made available to it to meet policy goals.

3.3 Administrative leadership

In many advanced states, the presence of an extensive legacy environment that was designed in silos, and which responded to each agency's particular demands or preferred technology environments, often slowed down implementation of e-government initiatives. This has required considerable investment to retrofit solutions to enable them to become interoperable.

Potentially, small states have less of a legacy problem than advanced information societies. This provides such countries with excellent opportunities to mobilise fast for e-government. Moreover, such a landscape will be less encumbered with power centres, by existing ICT cultures, by fixed mind-sets etc. This creates a unique opportunity as both the design process, as well as the subsequent implementation process, will be less subject to turf and resistance issues, ingrained positions and so on. Experience tends to show that major social and institutional reform programmes such as e-government have a far greater chance of success if they are embarked upon in a 'green field' environment, rather than in an environment that is lumbered by existing technologies, milieu etc.

3.3.1 Corporate governance framework

Lessons from advanced information societies have shown a correlation between the success of e-government and the presence of a corporate governance framework. Therefore governments have sought to consolidate policy decisions in this regard within the centre.

The administrative mechanisms to achieve this are various. Some jurisdictions have consolidated authority within central agencies, while others have moved towards a hybrid approach. The latter approach has resulted in the introduction of the *Office of the Chief Information Officer for Government*, supported by a network of chief information officers within each ministry portfolio.

The Chief Information Officer for Government is provided with full authority on all corporate aspects that relate to ICT – which also includes e-government. Responsibilities generally relate to architecture, standards, security, interoperability, single connectivity highways, consolidated technology environments etc.

However, chief information officers (CIOs) assigned to ministries are provided with full authority for ICT in their respective ministries in so far that they act within the corporate policy, standards and architecture directions established by the centre. Moreover, the CIOs act as e-champions on the behalf of the central authority within their respective ministries. In order to ensure that CIOs do not create separate fiefdoms and that they implement corporate directives, they are accountable to the Chief Information Officer for Government for such matters – while continuing to be accountable to the appropriate permanent secretary for ministry-specific ICT activity.

CIOs should delegate authority within a controlled environment. For a major programme such as the implementation of e-government, a *Programme Management Office* should be established within the Office of the Chief Information Officer for Government. The purpose of a Programme Management Office is to ensure that multiple project performances and implementation of the e-government programme are handled as effectively and as efficiently as possible, to ensure that projects are delivered within time, within budget and within the quality level established.

Box 3.2 Main aims of programme management

- Set out lines of responsibility and accountability within the Authority for the delivery of the project

- Give stakeholders in the Authority the ability to manage their interest in the project

- Support the Authority's project team to deliver the required outcomes by providing resources, giving direction and enabling trade-offs and timely decision-taking

- Provide a forum for issue resolution

- Provide access to best practice and independent expert advice

- Disseminate information by reporting to stakeholders so that they can effectively fulfil their roles

- Provide a framework for monitoring and evaluation, and project disclosures

Source: HM Treasury 2007

Small states, due to their size and constraints, may have gaps in highly-skilled human capital. Therefore, the creation of agencies with specific mandates may result in a situation where resources are too far stretched to create a sustainable mass. Moreover, this could also lead to the fragmentation of resources between programmes and ministries, as well as the scenario where programmes become dependent on individuals and the departure of a key individual may result in delay or collapse. Thus, it is considered to be far more appropriate if the information society, e-government and corporate technological components are integrated within one organisational entity.

3.4 Consultation with stakeholders

A reform can only succeed if the stakeholders that it will affect buy into said reform and own the process of implementation. E-government is a major transformation process. It not only affects how government interacts with its citizens, but also how citizens interact with government.

Too often, the government is seen as a monolithic entity. It is not; it is an institution constituted of sub-institutions with numerous government entities in various forms and personalities: departments, authorities, corporations, special operating entities, agencies etc. Every single entity has its own set of priorities and turf to manage, administer – and protect. What is more, governments may be organised on a multi-tiered basis: federal, regional and local. The challenges that each tier of government face differ from tier to tier, as well as within tiers.

Neither is the 'citizen' a faceless representation of society. Younger members of society are likely to be more ICT literate than elderly people. Youths in urban communities are also likely to have a higher degree of literacy than their counterparts in rural communities.

The above is a light overview of the multitude of stakeholders that will be affected by an e-government transformation process. The priorities of stakeholders will differ, as will expectations of the desired outcomes. Thus, consultation should be at the heart of both the design of an e-government strategy, as well as during the implementation of the strategy.

3.4.1 The working group
If appropriate to the social and political culture, the government should delegate drafting of the e-government strategy to a working group. This could consist of internal stakeholders only or joint government and external stakeholders. Such an approach will graft consultation within the design process, as consensus would be required for that strategy to be presented to government with the unanimous consent of all those involved.

The working group assigned responsibility for drafting the e-government strategy should undertake a broad consultation process, including as many stakeholders as possible, in order to graft into the document views, concerns and solutions as they arise. In this regard, there are various forms of consultation approaches that can be adopted. The extent and depth of the consultation process during this stage depends on the profile that the government wishes to place on the e-government strategy.

Box 3.3 Working group consultative process

The consultative process could include:

- The undertaking of surveys across a cohort of the population to identify which service citizens view as the most important to be addressed, and which delivery channel they are best prepared to use. The carrying out of such surveys will allow the designers to focus on priorities as citizens actually see them, rather than as the designers think they are – which is not necessarily the same. This will allow for a more immediate impact in the early stages of the e-government strategy implementation, as solutions are directed towards areas that are most frustrating to citizens.

- The undertaking of surveys across different types of enterprises – micro, small and medium enterprises (SMEs) and large – and to understand whether they are equipped to e-commerce (G2B) activity and identify issues, as well as identify the services they prioritise.

- The undertaking of focus groups with different cohorts of the public, both at citizen and entrepreneur levels – tourism, health, education, commerce etc. This will allow for further segmentation of sectoral expectations and hence for a more effective strategy design.

- The undertaking of workshops at ministry and agency levels within government, to understand the level of preparedness, what is realistic and doable in the immediate and short terms etc. This will assist in securing ownership of the strategy by the government's internal stakeholders.

- The undertaking of meetings with civil society and non-governmental organisations to obtain their views, particularly with regard to the 'soft' infrastructure issues.

- The holding of meetings with financial institutions to obtain their views on e-payment transactions.

- The holding of meetings with providers in the telecommunication markets to understand their concerns, the arising implications, and if their proposals for liberalisation can be carried out.

- The holding of meetings with regional offices or local councils to understand how they see themselves within an e-government framework.

3.4.2 Public consultation

Once the strategy has been designed, the government should publish it as a White Paper for public consultation. The White Paper should be made available to any person electronically from the main government website. However, the placement of a White Paper in the public domain is not in itself public consultation.

To secure public consultation, the government should synthesise the key parts of the e-government White Paper and make them available to every citizen by regular post. Furthermore, the government should use the media to bring the White Paper to the public's attention.

In tandem with communicating the White Paper through the media, the chair of the working group responsible for drafting the strategy should carry out a comprehensive 'road show' in order to hold discussions with as many stakeholders as possible. This can be achieved in a number of ways, which include holding meetings with the public, with constituted bodies representing different sectors and/or with civil society.

3.4.3 Final draft

It is imperative that once the feedback from the public consultation process triggered by the public issuance of the White Paper is received, this is not only analysed but – more importantly – communicated to the public.

Thus, the drafters of the strategy should subsequently review the original draft published as a White Paper and present a new draft to government, setting out departures from the original as well as a transparent assessment of the feedback received.

The government should publish the final draft of the e-government strategy, together with the feedback received. If the circumstances of the country permit, it should debate the strategy in parliament to obtain political consensus and ensure that e-government as a policy will be retained, as governments may change.

3.4.4 Implementation

Once the e-government strategy becomes policy, implementation commences. Implementation, however, is the start rather than the end of the journey. As mentioned earlier, the implementation of e-government is carried out over a generational horizon. This means that consultation does not stop once the implementation stage is initiated. Rather, the process of ensuring that key stakeholders constitute part of the implementation process, and are involved in the development of the information society, potentially assumes greater importance at this stage.

A strategic approach to e-government that embraces government, society, business and non-government organisations is more likely to succeed. Such an approach ensures that all of the key components that render e-government successful – affordability and accessibility, or e-literacy, for example – are brought together and developed in tandem with the technology framework necessary to promulgate e-government.

3.5 Financing e-government

Small states should consider placing the funds required to propel e-government forward with the central agency assigned responsibility for e-government. There are various advantages with regards to the adoption of such an approach. First, a central fund will provide a 'critical mass', which may not be possible if the financing for e-government is placed across many votes. This will allow for better planning and utilisation of funds, particularly with regards to ministerial cross-cutting initiatives.

Second, the establishment of a robust e-government framework requires time to achieve. Individual ministries or agencies may perceive this as a brake on introducing improvements within their respective domains. Frustration may bubble over into a separate and ad hoc approach.

Third, the key technological building blocks must be unified, consistent, coherent, standardised, inter-connected and based upon shared services. And fourth, the government's priorities in the roll-out of e-government may be directed towards one or more particular segments or cohorts of society or the economy. A central funding vote will ensure that focus in this regard will be maintained.

Box 3.4 Key e-government building blocks for centralised financing

- The setting up of the e-government middleware (that is software that mediates between the e/m delivery channel (tablet, desktop, smart phone, etc) and the back end applications) architecture and the e-government technological framework

- The setting up of the e-government payment gateway

- The setting up of the e-government security framework

- The setting up of the m-government gateway

- The setting up of the e-government portal

- The government process re-engineering exercises, both formal and virtual, that will have to take place

3.6 E-governance monitoring and evaluation

It is necessary to monitor and evaluate e-government to understand demand, assess the benefits to users of alternative proposals and evaluate the effectiveness of proposals in meeting their objectives. Evaluation is needed to argue the case for new projects and expenditure, to justify continuing with the initiatives, to allocate additional IT funds, to assess progress towards programme goals and to understand impacts. Additionally, monitoring and evaluation can assist with programme consolidation and selection of standards.

Following the prioritisation of e-governance as a key strategy to attain a particular national vision and strategic objectives, specific and measurable key performance indicators need to be identified in order to monitor and track progress towards stated objectives throughout the lifecycle of the project. E-government indicators should be designed to reflect programme goals, and a framework for monitoring and evaluation should be prepared prior to initiation.

A performance indicator or key performance indicator (KPI) is a term that denotes the *measure of performance*. KPIs are commonly used by a country or organisation to evaluate its success or the success of a particular activity in which it is engaged. Sometimes success is defined in terms of making progress toward strategic goals, but often success is simply the repeated achievement of some level of operational goal.

Accordingly, choosing the right KPIs is reliant upon having a good understanding of what is important to a particular sector of an organisation. Because of the need to develop a good understanding of what is important, performance indicator selection is often closely associated with the use of various techniques to assess the present state of the sector or business, and its key activities. These assessments often lead to the identification of potential improvements; and as a consequence, performance indicators are routinely associated with 'performance improvement' initiatives.

With regards to e-government, a country may seek to tie its KPIs with international benchmarks, or design an internal KPI framework that is directed towards what it identifies as key priorities. International frameworks are often indices made up of multiple performance indicators, which can provide more precise measures of governance than single indicators and allow for cross-country comparisons, but are dependent upon the availability of data on robust indicators.

An example of an international e-government KPI framework is the United Nations' E-Government Development Index (EGDI). The EGDI is built around a number of indexes: the telecommunication infrastructure index; the human capital index; and the supplementary e-participation index.

The E-Government Development Index (EGDI) is a comprehensive scoring of the willingness and capacity of national administrations to use online and mobile technology in the execution of government functions. The EGDI is not designed to capture e-government development, but rather rates the performance of national governments relative to one another. While the methodological framework for the EGDI has remained consistent across survey periods, survey questions are adjusted to reflect evolving knowledge of best practices in e-government, changes in technology and other factors, and data collection practices have been periodically refined (UN 2012).

As stated, international benchmarks provide a reference with regards to how a country is proceeding with the implementation of e-government relative to other countries. However, they do not provide a framework against which a particular country can spur implementation, gauge progress, identify gaps and take corrective measures. To achieve this, a government would need to design its own national e-government KPI framework.

The breadth and depth of a KPI framework can be as broad and as deep as the government needs it to be. Thus, if the government wants to establish a holistic KPI framework, it would need to target five primary areas:

1) ICT supply

2) ICT demand

3) ICT products

4) ICT infrastructure

5) Information and electronic content

Nevertheless, it is not recommended that a country introduces a holistic KPI framework at the outset of the e-government implementation process. This is primarily for two reasons. First, such a holistic framework is ambitious and will require considerable resources from the entity responsible for national statistics. Second, the indicators required in the early stages are potentially different to those required during the middle part of the implementation process, which again will be different to the indicators required as the e-government process matures.

An evolutionary approach that starts small and is focused, and which over time evolves into a holistic KPI framework, would potentially add more value.

Initially, the e-government KPI framework could be introduced to target key components of the strategy.

Figure 3.1 A general framework to organise indicators

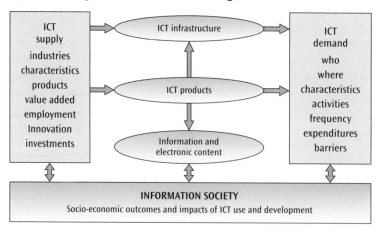

Source: Spiezia 2010

**Figure 3.2 Approach to indicator development to measure the
e-government implementation process**

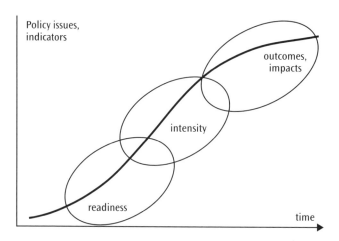

3.7 ICT capacity building

In the information age, knowledge is power. The knowledge economy is based on a paradigm that focuses on intellectual capital as a prime mover. With knowledge replacing physical and natural resources as the key ingredient in economic development, education and human resource development policies require rethinking. While there is no standard definition of a 'knowledge economy' as such, the UK Department of Trade and Industry defined it as 'a knowledge-driven economy in which the generation and exploitation of knowledge play the predominant role in the creation of wealth'

(Bedford 2013: 279) Meanwhile, the OECD defined a knowledge economy as 'an economy that is directly based on the production, distribution and use of knowledge and information' (Mustafa and Abdullah 2004: 51).

Investment in human capital is critical in a knowledge economy. Education and training are fundamental to the widespread and effective use of new technologies. Since a networked society is essentially a knowledge society, many of the potential benefits of ICT relate directly to the capability to use data and information to create new knowledge. Therefore, human resources development is considered to be a core component of an ICT strategy and one of the most challenging bottlenecks for developing countries seeking to engage successfully in e-business.

In many developing countries, the literacy rate is low, especially among women and girls, and the level of education is insufficient for full implementation of the changes in work organisation that are required for the efficient adoption of ICT. Given the relatively fast technological change related to ICT, continuous learning is required. This means that even adults need to improve skills or acquire new ones on a regular basis (UNCTAD 2003).

Human capital theory views education and training as an investment that can yield social and private returns, through increased knowledge and skills for economic development and social progress. The economic argument in favour of knowledge-based education and training is linked to the perceived needs of the global economy. It is based on the assumption that economic growth and development are knowledge driven and human capital dependent.

Additionally, evidence shows that a nation's ability to prosper is correlated to its level, quality and application of IT. Thus, a country that does not mobilise its resources to transform its society into an ICT society will get caught in a digital divide when compared to a similar country that does successfully transform its society into an ICT-literate one.

Moreover, unless businesses and consumers are educated about the opportunities and benefits offered by ICT, and unless they are trained to use the internet, e-business will not take off. While access to computers and the internet is essential, it is not enough. It is equally vital to create a demand for the new technologies and for e-commerce. Some have even argued that education, and not connectivity, is the main challenge for most developing countries seeking to participate in the digital economy.

Transforming a society into an ICT-literate one requires a series of measures – both in the short term and long term.

3.7.1 Short-term strategies

Immediate action can be taken to increase the level of ICT literacy. One effective measure is the establishment of an accredited ICT level of education, and the provision of free or highly-subsidised tuition to citizens in both rural and urban communities to obtain said accreditation/certification. The attainment ICT accreditation can also be spurred by establishing such accreditation as a mandatory criterion to enter employment with government.

The attainment of industry-specific accreditations, such as CISCO, Microsoft and other such accreditations, will be expensive if the training delivery channels are not present in the country or are run on purely a private sector basis. Governments should seek to enter into vertical partnerships with industry players so that they establish academies with a government institution and/or NGO to deliver training for their respective industry accreditations at affordable local rates.

Such measures will assist in securing a high degree of ICT literacy, particularly with regard to people entering the labour market for the first time or those who are already active participants. The government should ensure that its senior employees are trained in information management, as well as the business application of ICT.

3.7.2 Long-term strategies

For ICT to become part of the milieu of a country's society, a more pervasive and fundamental approach is required. In essence, the education system across the primary, secondary and tertiary levels will need to be reformed in order to leverage ICT as a tool for education, as well as to integrate ICT within the country's curriculum.

ICT itself is an important tool for education. Indeed it brings in a new ethos (Camilleri 1994); for example:

- it enriches existing areas of the curriculum by improving their nature and content;

- it facilitates teaching and learning by helping teachers and students to concentrate on high-level, non-routine cognitive tasks;

- it provides a platform for collaborative learning, as well as virtually joining classes with other schools within and outside the country;

- it promotes active, rather than passive, learning;

- it increases interaction through sound, video, animation etc.; and

- it exponentially opens up access to research resources.

> ### Box 3.5 UNESCO's ICT in Education Policy-makers' Toolkit
>
> The UN Educational, Scientific and Cultural Organization's (UNESCO) ICT in Education Toolkit provides education strategists with six toolboxes – containing a total of 18 tools – that cover the following areas:
>
> 1. Mapping the present situation in terms of national goals, educational context, ICT in education and the dynamics of change
>
> 2. Identification of educational areas for ICT intervention and formulation of corresponding ICT in Education policies
>
> 3. Planning for implementation of infrastructure, hardware and personnel training
>
> 4. Planning for content
>
> 5. Consolidating implementation plans and their financial and managerial implications into one master plan
>
> 6. Assessment of implementation, effectiveness and impact of ICT interventions and subsequent adjustments and follow-up actions
>
> **Source:** UNESCO 2006

3.7.3 IT in primary and secondary education

The use of ICT for education purposes should not be confused with the provision of computer or ICT studies. The use of ICT for education means the provision of learning through the utilisation of ICT as a tool – today termed as 'e-learning'. However, a number of foundation stones need to be put in place in order to leverage ICT for education.

First is the training of teachers who will be affected by the resulting necessary changes in curriculum and methodology – particularly those teachers who are already in service. In-service training could be directed as follows:

- the provision of IT training so that teachers who are not IT literate obtain the appropriate level of competency; and

- the provision of training in the use of IT as a teaching and learning resource within their particular area of specialisation.

With regard to students who are learning to become teachers, the appropriate university or teachers' college should review their curriculum to introduce the relevant modules so that students will graduate with appropriate knowledge in the use of IT for education.

Second, is the pedagogical content to be used for e-learning. The design of pedagogical content is challenging and should not be underestimated. Courseware may be available and secured through inter-school agreements with foreign schools, and perhaps in certain subjects it may be used with little customisation (mathematics, physics, etc.). However, this may not be the case with other subjects, or the way ready-made courseware is designed may not be applicable for the country in question. Introducing ICT for education without the appropriate pedagogical content is unlikely to succeed. It is also difficult to expect each school or a teacher to develop such content on their own stream. A particular way forward would be to create an e-learning unit within the central entity responsible for education. This unit will be responsible for the preparation of the content, as well for training teachers in the use of the content through ICT tools.

The third of the foundation stones that need to be in place in order to leverage e-learning is that teachers should be provided with a laptop computer, which will serve as the medium through which they will prepare and deliver their lectures. Most international computer companies provide special rates for equipment and licences used for educational purposes. Negotiations should be conducted with local agents to secure good value for money deals in this regard.

Fourth, the gradual introduction of IT for education should be supported by a review of the national education curriculum. IT could be viewed as a platform for a radical change in curricular activity, to support group work and fast and easy access to knowledge in its various forms.

Fifth, students are to be provided access to technology and the internet. Access to technology can be provided in various ways – the placement of a number PCs in every class, the establishment of computing laboratories, the establishment of a number of designated e-learning classrooms, converting school libraries into an IT access library etc. Moreover, students should be provided with an email address to allow them to interact electronically with one another and their teachers, as well as a 'My Learning' web space where they can electronically lodge their homework, assignments and other material relating to school activity. Access to the internet should be through a gateway that creates a 'Chinese wall' against full web availability, thereby ensuring access to only those sites which will be designated as appropriate by the central education agency. Specialised web filters for school purposes exist and can be procured at a relatively low cost.

Box 3.6   Red Enlaces: ten years of IT education in Chile

Launched by Chile's Ministry of Education in 1992, the Enlaces programme is an example of one of the early efforts by a government to prepare students for the information society and to introduce ICT into a country's basic education system. The programme provides infrastructure (computers and internet access), capacity building (for teachers) and content (educational software and websites). Enlacesa is the main provider of ICT equipment in the country's schools; in 2001, it provided 80 per cent of equipment in primary schools and 59 per cent in secondary schools.

In 2008, at least 87 per cent of the school body in Chile had access to ICT thanks to this initiative; with an expected ratio of 10 students per computer (2010), one of the most crucial aspects of Enlaces is its appropriate educational content which includes the Chilean curriculum – supported by the state educational portal (http://ict4bop.wordpress.com/2012/02/09/ict-and-education-in-chile).

The programme aims not only to provide access to the internet and new technologies, but also to introduce the use of ICT into school curricula as a support medium for teaching. Results in this area have been limited thus far, since the programme has mainly focused on training staff members to use the system, rather than encouraging teachers to use ICT as a pedagogical tool. This remains one of the most important challenges for the future development of the programme.

The measures discussed above are not short-term activities. They will take a generation to achieve. This means that the process of implementation will have to be gradual and prioritised. Prioritisation will reflect a country's culture and norms. Should the focus be initially directed towards students in the last year of upper or secondary school, and roll-out subsequently implemented with regards to secondary school to fourth, third etc. grades? Or should implementation be directed towards students in primary school? An advantage of a primary school-based approach, particularly in a country where a family gives considerable importance and attention to a child's education, is that it will have a ripple effect on the parents. As parents sit with their child or children, they too will become exposed to IT.

3.7.4 IT in higher institutions

The role that higher institutions play with regards to inculcating IT literacy is different from that played by primary and secondary institutions. Whilst the latter is primarily concerned with the development of an IT literate society by ensuring that students during their formative years are armed with the appropriate skills to successfully manipulate the electronic age and the knowledge economy, the role of higher institutions is directed towards the development of skills to meet demand and supply of IT labour.

Too often, IT education at higher institutions is directed towards preparing students to follow specialised IT degrees at an undergraduate level. IT, however, has rapidly grown into a field that transcends traditional disciplines. This means that an effective education strategy to build IT labour skills that will service the labour market must be two-pronged.

The first prong is the delivery of technical IT skills. Technical colleges should deliver industry-accredited programmes, as students who follow such accreditation or certified programmes are then 'industry' prepared. They are likely to find employment, as employers have no need to invest in order to orient such a skilled individual to a particular technical or software-based position.

The second prong should be directed towards the building of appropriate capacity within a university in relation to encouraging IT proficiency in every discipline, as well as targeting key IT disciplines. A university with an IT Department should maintain strong links with the IT business sector, to ensure that it is producing graduates in disciplines and with the level of knowledge required by industry.

3.7.5 IT in government

The possibility exists that as an IT industry starts to develop, the supply of IT human capital in a country is not sufficient and will not meet local needs under normal circumstances. In the event that supply is scarce, industry will start to poach employees from one another. Inevitably, the cost of labour will rise. This could be damaging to an emerging, indigenous IT industry.

A potential solution in this regard is for government to enter the training market over and above its normal education streams discussed above, by establishing public–private partnerships with private industry trainers in order to boost training infrastructure.

Such a strategic move, which should be temporary in nature, may be beneficial to the country, particularly when the IT industry is at its most vulnerable. This is because it will bring the focused resources of both government and the private sector to increase the supply of IT labour, and in doing so will stabilise the IT labour market.

The government should ensure that its senior employees are trained in information management, as well as the business application of ICT. Too often, people who occupy senior positions in government are 50 years and over – particularly if the selection criteria is that of seniority. The older the person who occupies a senior position is, the higher the possibility that such a person will be unfamiliar with the management aspects of ICT.

A direct consequence of this is that too often the investment made in ICT is not maximised beyond the basic processing transactions of the application. Yet the data resident within a system and across systems provides valuable information, which if maximised should improve the intelligence that is so important in the design of a policy instrument.

3.8 Conclusion: keys to overcoming challenges

The challenges that policy-makers will face and will need to overcome are many. They include, though are not limited to, the need to obtain political support, maintaining that support over time as policy priorities change, and securing continuity in government financing in the face of shifting policy priorities and times when the economy may be facing difficulties.

Furthermore, key challenges in many e-government projects include:

- unrealistic project design and goals;

- lack of time spent on planning and design;

- lack of clear and measurable project goals, objectives and anticipated benefits;

- minimal focus on key project enablers (e.g. GPR, people change, capacity building);

- poor communication to stakeholders and users on objectives and benefits;

- inadequate resources for the project (in terms of people and funding);

- lack of capacity to conceptualise and manage e-government projects;

- minimal leadership and prioritising of e-government initiatives; and

- lack of stable and permanent project leadership with managerial powers to drive projects.

In order to address the above-discussed challenges, a comprehensive approach for conceptualisation, implementation and maintenance of an e-governance project is required. Such an approach would support government to: get it right the first time; orient project designs with customer focus and needs; achieve heightened focus and prioritisation of business and stakeholder benefits; support the adoption of best fit practices; and to manage delivery of results.

References

Bedford, Denise AD (2013), 'Expanding the Definition and Measurement of Knowledge Economy: Integrating Triple Bottom Line Factors into Knowledge Economy Index Models and Methodologies', *Journal of Modern Accounting and Auditing*, Vol 9, No 2, 278–286, www.davidpublishing.com/davidpublishing/Upf ile/4/1/2013/2013040101564342.pdf (accessed 17 April 2013).

Camilleri, J (2004), 'A National Strategy for Information Technology for Malta', Office of the National Strategy for Information Technology, University of Malta, October.

HM Treasury (2007), *Project governance: a guidance note for public sector projects*, November 2007, Crown copyright, Norwich.

Mustapha, R, and A Abdullah (2004), 'Malaysia Transitions Toward a Knowledge-Based Economy', *Journal of Technology Studies*, Vol. 30 Issue 3, available at: http://scholar.lib.vt.edu/ejournals/JOTS/v30/v30n3/pdf/mustapha.pdf (accessed 17 April 2013).

OECD (2005), OECD e-Government Studies: Norway 2005, available at: www.oecd-ilibrary.org/governance/oecd-e-government-studies_19901054 (accessed 17 April 2013).

Parisopoluous, K, E Tambouris and K Tarabanis (2007), 'Analyzing and Comparing European eGovernment Strategies', World Bank: Washington, DC.

Spiezia, V (2010), *Setting International Standards for ICT Indicators: An overview of the OECD Working Party on Indicators for the Information Society*, Directorate for Science, Technology and Industry, OECD, Paris, 29–30 March, available at: www.oecd.org/gov/public-innovation/45072149.pdf (accessed 17 April 2013).

United Nations (2012), *United Nations e-Government Survey 2012: E-Government for the People*, United Nations Department of Economic and Social Affairs. UN: New York.

UNCTAD (2003), E-Commerce and Development Report, United Nations Conference on Trade and Development, UNCTAD/SIDTE/ECB/2003/12003.

UNESCO (2006), 'UNESCO ICT in Education Policy Makers' Toolkit', UNESCO Bangkok, available at: www.unescobkk.org/fr/education/ict/ict-in-education-projects/policy/toolkit (accessed 17 April 2013).

Chapter 4

Government Process Re-engineering

Tony Ming

While the previous chapters highlighted the potential of e-governance to increase the efficiency of government operations, this will not necessarily deliver the best results or increase citizen-centricity until processes are reconfigured and redesigned. Therefore, the process of government process re-engineering is an important element of successful e-governance.

4.1 What is GPR?

There are many schools of thought on how to carry out public sector transformation. Business process re-engineering (BPR), redefined as government process re-engineering (GPR), involves a quantum leap in organisational transformation rather than incremental improvements.

As defined by Dr Michael Hammer, one of the founders of the management theory of BPR,

> Business Process Re-engineering is the *fundamental reconsideration* and *radical redesign* of organisational processes, in order to achieve *dramatic improvements* of current performance in *cost, speed, and quality of service* (Hammer 1990).

GPR is the application of re-engineering within a government context; however, the underlying principles of BPR are universal:

- **Fundamental reconsideration** – This goes back to the raison d'être of the organisation and asks questions such as: Should government be operating in this industry? Could this function be conducted better outside government? Is this a core business for government?

- **Radical redesign** – 'Thinking outside the box' becomes part of the critical thinking process and the focus is on the customer. There are several techniques that could be applied to conduct a radical redesign and these will be covered in more detail later in the chapter.

- **Dramatic improvements** – Quantum leaps in improvement in cost, time and speed are associated with GPR initiatives. In some instances, breakthrough improvements are established initially and incremental changes are applied on an ongoing basis to further refine redesigned processes.

4.2 Why is GPR necessary?

For GPR to be successful, the organisation must have a compelling reason to change.

Governments have been forced to change due to the global financial crisis. A significant source of public revenues in developing countries is foreign remittances, and as a result of the crisis remittances have reduced significantly due to higher levels of unemployment in countries that employ immigrants. The growing and unsustainable budget deficit – further exacerbated by increased levels of spending due to a rise in demand for social programmes – is pressuring government to become more efficient and reduce costs of operation, while improving customer service.

E-government is a growing priority within government, where public services are being demanded by citizens and the private sector on a '24/7/365' basis. E-government also increases governance and transparency, transforming government to be more responsive to the needs of citizens and more transparent to assess the performance of government. At the same time, e-government services reduce the costs of transacting with government. However, e-government cannot operate within current bureaucratic and 'silo' organisations, since it requires full and seamless integration and co-ordination of ministries to process digital transactions that require the attention of more than one department.

Many small island states depend on foreign direct investment as a major source of revenues, and they are being pressured to provide e-government services to reduce red tape and decrease the cost of doing business – for example, to retain and attract offshore banking companies. This industry has competition from around the globe and, without such organisational improvements, businesses will relocate to countries that are more business-friendly. Modern infrastructure, the internet, social networks and mobile telephones are being utilised to enhance the investment climate, attracting investors and making government more efficient and competitive.

This provides a sample of the business rationale for undertaking a dramatic transformation of government – it is not optional, but mandatory.

4.3 GPR methodology

The framework in Figure 4.1 provides an overview of the re-engineering process, which will be discussed in more detail later on. The framework is based on the author's experience of re-engineering a variety of government departments in the Caribbean and North America.

4.3.1 Impetus for change

Since GPR involves radical change, it is imperative to define a persuasive reason for undertaking such an initiative. The reason provides the basis for change management

Figure 4.1 Process re-engineering framework

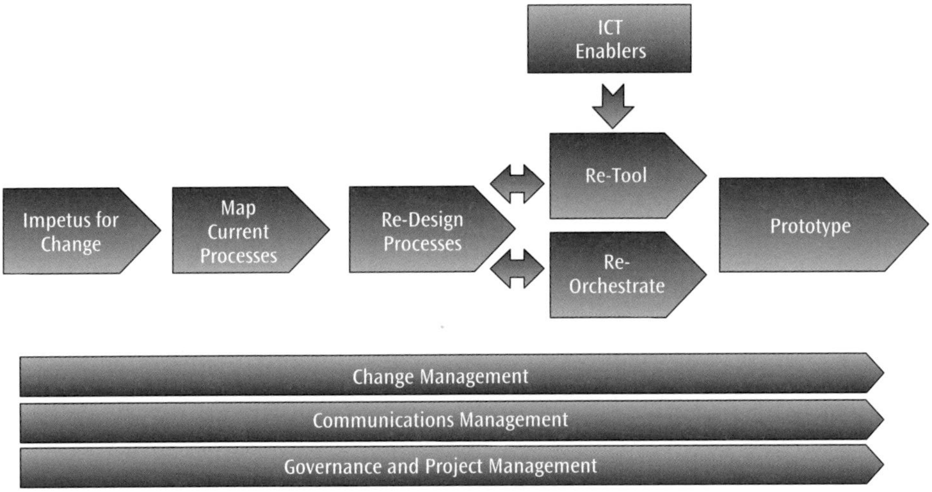

Source: Ming 2012: 38

activities, where staff must be sold on the new way of doing business and stakeholders need to understand the underlying rationale for change.

In addition to a compelling reason, a strong and influential sponsor is required to lead the GPR initiative. Although GPR may be seen in some circles as a technology project, it is truly a government transformation process that must be led and driven by a non-ICT ministry or sponsor.

4.3.2 Mapping current processes

Conducting an exercise to understand and map the current situation helps to identify where the inefficiencies and bottlenecks are occurring, and the reasons behind these problems. It also provides a baseline to measure the level of improvements that have occurred at the end of the GPR exercise, and whether the GPR targets have been achieved. The key outputs from this phase are: a map of the current processes; metrics for costs, time and quality; and rules that govern the processing of the trigger, or the event that initiates the process.

Although there are a variety of techniques to map processes, a useful one is swim lanes, a tool that identifies activities conducted in each department. This technique provides a visual that shows how the trigger is processed by different departments, how hand-offs (persons involved in the process) occur and the time the trigger spends in each department. Figure 4.2 provides an example of this.

Figure 4.2 An example of mapping current processes: tax department returns processing

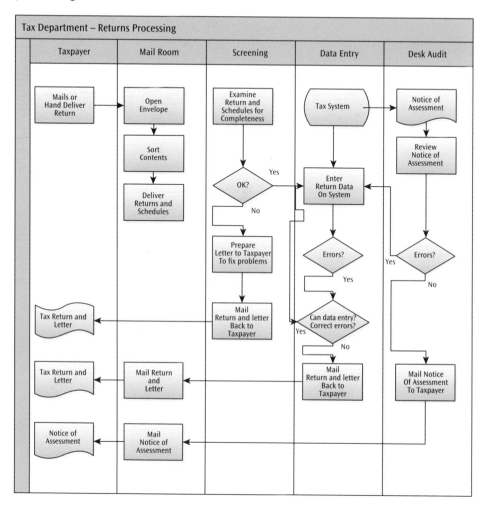

4.3.3 Re-designing processes

The basic premise for the redesign phase is to develop processes that are customer focused, efficient and reduce the number of hand-offs. The outputs from this phase are: redesign options, evaluation of options through selection criteria and a map of the new redesigned processes that will meet the targets that have been set for the GPR initiative. It is important to understand that this phase drives the technological solution that will meet the needs of the redesigned processes. In addition, redesigned processes shape the organisation design and identify legislative changes that are required to support the new processes.

There are a variety of techniques that could be applied to redesign processes:

- **Utopia pull** – This involves starting with a blank sheet of paper to design the optimal process, without taking into consideration any constraints. Then constraints are applied that cannot be re-engineered away – for instance, cultural, financial or capacity constraints. The result is a process has been designed that provides an optimal solution to deal with efficiencies, and meets the targets that have been set for the project.

- **Enlightenment** – This avoids the 'was not invented here' syndrome. Instead of starting from scratch, borrow what other countries have successfully implemented, learning from their mistakes and adopting best practices. This will reduce costs and timelines for the project, as processes will be mature and bugs would have been resolved. For example, the requirements and data architecture for tax systems are universal. All tax jurisdictions require a tax roll, returns processing, payment processing, a risk management system, audit, appeals and compliance. There is no need to reinvent the wheel.

- **Rule-busting** – This is probably one of the most common redesigning techniques. Many processes are governed by rules that have been around for many years and are part of an organisation's policy or procedures, but have outlived their usefulness. If a rule is causing bottlenecks and undue delays in processing, it should be reviewed and where necessary modified or eliminated. For example, an old rule that all corporate registration applications have to be completed in triplicate with hard copies to ensure that backup copies are available in the event that the original is lost, is not necessary in the twenty-first century with the advent of technology. This rule could be eliminated.

- **Reduce hand-offs** – Every time there is a hand-off, a delay occurs since it sits in an inbox until the employee has time to address the trigger. In addition, the further away processing occurs from the customer, the greater the chances are for inaccurate information to be captured, more rejects to occur and processing delays to increase. Information should be captured at source and employees empowered to make decisions.

- **Parallel processing** – Many triggers are processed sequentially, as each trigger moves from one department to another. If the trigger was processed by a team, then the team could collaborate and work in parallel to process the transaction. This will reduce the turnaround time to process the transaction, will reduce costs and improve customer service.

- **Before or after** – Many governments insist on processing the whole trigger before a confirmation is provided to the customer. The key idea with this option is to focus on the customer and find ways to increase the speed to complete the transaction. In some instances where the risk is not significant, this may be appropriate – for instance, where the transaction is partially processed; a confirmation is issued; and then later the transaction process can be completed, as in the example in Box 4.1.

Box 4.1 Before and after

A government requires the applicant for a corporate registration to file a 10-page application together with 15 pages of supporting documentation. Under the old system, it takes about four months to process the application and issue the registration number. In the meantime, the applicant cannot open a bank account and start up his or her business.

The new process reduces the number of pages on the application form to five, while the supporting documentation is reduced to nine pages. If the application is completed correctly, then a preliminary corporate registration number is issued so that the registrant could go about opening his/her business. The supporting documentation would be reviewed later on a random basis and also according to risk characteristics. If there are no problems, then the registrant is notified that the preliminary number is now permanent. If problems occur, then the number is revoked and, depending on the severity of the problem, a significant penalty could be levied. The end result is that the business operator could start business within two days instead of four months. Further improvements could be obtained by e-filing the registration form.

4.3.4 Evaluating and selecting suitable projects

There are a variety of methodologies to assess suitable project options, which could be classified into two categories: *tangible benefits* and *intangible benefits*.

Tangible benefits

Net present value (NVP) is used to rank projects. It is calculated by establishing net cash flows (inflows less outflows), determining the discount rate and discounting cash flows for each year:

(net cash flows) / *((1 + discount rate)*^{time}*)*

If NVP ≤ 0 then the project would be rejected; if NVP is > 0 then the project could be invested in. The project with the highest NVP would be given the highest priority. This is exemplified in Table 4.1.

Table 4.1 Net present value calculation example

Year	Amount	Discount rate	Discount factor	Discounted net cash flows
0 – investment	($5,000,000)			
1	$1,000,000	10%	.909	$909,000
2	$2,000,000	10%	.826	$1,652,000
3	$2,000,000	10%	.751	$1,502,000
4	($1,000,000)	10%	.683	($683,000)
5	$3,000,000	10%	.621	$1,863,000
Totals				$5,243,000

Notes:
NPV = $5,243,000 – ($5,000,000) = $243,000
NPV > 0 therefore accept project

While this technique enables a robust economic evaluation of the project and is used widely in the public and private sectors, it is difficult to explain to decision-makers and it is also often difficult to estimate cash flows and the discount rate.

Payback period is technique used to rank projects based on the number of years it would take to pay back their investment. It is established through calculating the net cash flows for each year, subtracting net cash flows for each year from the investment, and then calculating the number of years or partial years it would take to pay back the investment.

The desired number of years for the project to pay back investment should first be established – typically for ICT projects this should be less than five years. If the actual payback is less than the target payback, then the project should be invested in. If the actual payback is more than the target, then the project should be rejected. The project with the lowest payback period is ranked as the highest priority. Table 4.2 shows an example of the payback period calculation.

Although this technique is simple to understand and explain, it does not take into consideration the time value of cash flows and also ignores cash flows after the payback period.

Table 4.2 Payback period calculation example

Year	Amount	Remaining balance
0 – investment	($5,000,000)	
1	$1,000,000	($4,000,000)
2	$2,000,000	($2,000,000)
3	$2,000,000	0
4	($1,000,000)	
5	$2,000,000	
Totals		

Notes: Payback period = 3 years

Intangible benefits

Where it is difficult to quantify benefits, Table 4.3 provides a fairly simple methodology to evaluate each project and select the option that best meets the needs of the customer.

Table 4.3 Project evaluation methodology

Projects	Customer benefits				Organisation benefits					Aversion factors			
	Quality	Speed	Convenience	Others	Operational savings	Productivity	Strategic advantage	Prestige	Others	Implementation cost	Difficulty	Project risk	Others
Project 1	+++	+++	++		+	++	+++	+++		---	---	---	
Project 2	--	--	---		+++	+++	---	---		-	---	--	
Project 3													

Source: National University of Singapore eGL Business Process Re-engineering workshop material 2009.

4.3.5 Re-tooling

The overall objective of re-tooling is to conduct an environmental scan to identify technology solutions that will satisfy the requirements of the redesigned processes. It should be stressed that requirements drive technology solutions, and not the other way around.

Technology is the key enabler to re-engineering initiatives, since it introduces new ways of doing business and disrupts the current way of processing triggers. The introduction of 'disruptive technologies' such as the internet, mobile devices, Web 2.0/3.0 and cloud computing has revolutionised how government organisations operate.

The **internet** is a ubiquitous tool that allows government to provide services 24/7/365 that are accessible to all. Instead of customers having to deal with arduous travel, hours of queuing, processing fees and long waits, the internet provides a vehicle where the customer can use a service at any time in the comfort of their homes – reducing the costs to the customer and significantly improving customer service. The internet also creates a facility to allow government to be more transparent through publishing public data online, therefore increasing social accountability.

The number of **mobile devices** is increasing exponentially; the International Telecommunication Union projects that by 2015 there will be enough mobile phones for each of the 7 billion citizens in the world. This phenomenon provides the opportunity for governments to 'leapfrog' the technology gap in developing countries. Simple mobile devices can be purchased for less than US$20, and this simple technology can be used to provide a wealth of services. In India, a database was created by farmers to register labourers who were interested in harvesting crops. When a farmer needs labourers, an SMS message is sent to the relevant labourers notifying them of the job and the location of the farm that requires their services. Previously, labourers had to go through a middleman and pay a commission to obtain a job from the farmer (eFarmDirect 2012).

Technological innovations complement GPR and can be employed to build high-level technology architecture in government – including application systems, data and infrastructure – as well as make government processes more open and available to citizens.

4.3.6 Re-orchestration

The key objectives in this phase are to align the organisation structure, new job descriptions, performance management systems and supporting legislation with the redesigned processes.

Re-engineering will result in changes to the way that ministries/departments are organised. The removal of 'silos' to allow teams to function will result in changes in structures from discrete functional departments into multi-faceted teams that are designed around processes – not around departments or activities.

Similarly, changes in legislation may be required to support the new processes since old rules will be eliminated to streamline antiquated processes. To ensure that the new way of doing business is institutionalised, new performance management systems are necessary to ensure that the right incentives are incorporated into performance contracts.

The outputs of re-orchestration include a new organisational design, legislative changes, a training plan and strategy, new job descriptions, new reward structures and the requirements for factors of production.

Re-tooling and re-orchestration enables the creation of a roadmap to achieve a certain vision. This prototype of new processes includes specific, measurable, attainable, relevant and time-bound (SMART) projects and monitoring and evaluation tools for these projects, ready for implementation.

4.4 Management of GPR

GPR must be led by a strong and influential non-ICT ministry or sponsor. In addition to providing resources to the GPR team, this sponsor is required to be the executive champion who will liaise with his/her peers to obtain buy-in, deal with territorial issues, negotiate with senior executives and drive the project to completion. Without a strong sponsor the probability of success will be low, because the biggest challenge in GPR is change management.

> **E-government in Malta** was initially under the leadership of the prime minister. This was because multiple ministries were to be impacted, and therefore the initiative required a strong central leader to deal with cross-ministry issues. Once the e-government initiative was underway, then an e-Government Office was created and placed within the Ministry of ICT.

Management focus will be on being a coach rather than supervising, as teams should be self-managed and empowered to make decisions. Core management functions are to ensure that change, communication and project management functions are fully considered and to ensure that processes and methodologies for these are in place. These include change and communications strategies, a project management governance structure and organisation of project management.

4.5 Change management

E-government is not about technology, but rather about changing norms, behaviour, attitudes and culture. Getting people to shift from their 'comfort zone' to an unfamiliar place requires discipline, dedication and, above all else, commitment from all levels of management. Change management is probably the most difficult aspect of GPR.

Resistance to an implementation of an e-government strategy from within the public service is to be expected. Resistance to change – both individual and

Figure 4.3 GPR project structure

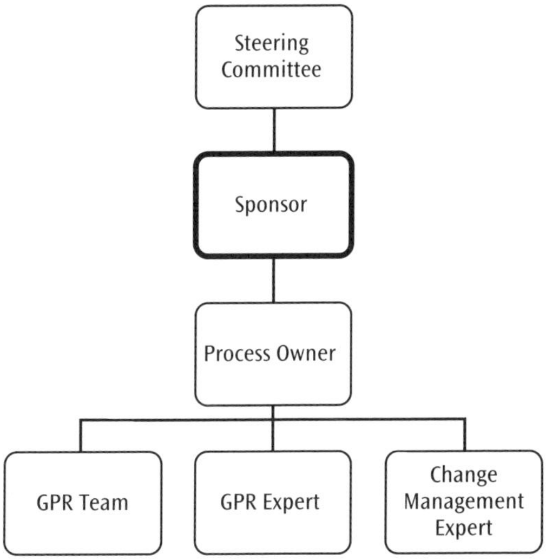

organisational – arises for a variety of reasons, including fear, scepticism, concern, inertia or for economic factors. The key is that such resistance should be anticipated strategically, planned for and subsequently managed. People need to know why change is necessary, what the benefits are and how they will be affected.

Change fails, in most instances, because the change process is not managed. There are many change management models floating around; however, there are key elements to any change process:

- **Clear vision** – the destination must be clearly defined with a road map that charts the course to be taken

- **Compelling reason** – there has to be urgency in GPR initiatives, with disastrous consequences for inaction

- **Commitment from the top** – a strong coalition with influential leaders is required to set the right example and drive change within the organisation

- **Quick wins** – identify 'low hanging fruit' and deliver these successes quickly to build momentum, credibility and demonstrate tangible progress

- **Continuous communication** – constant communication with staff and key stakeholders is necessary to obtain buy-in and address concerns

- **Institutionalise change** – to sustain change it must be inculcated into the processes of the entire organisation

Performance management schemes should ensure that the new government model is rewarded and 'no change' behaviour is questioned.

Some organisations have good intentions initially as they embark on the GPR journey; however, many have applied re-engineering in a superficial manner, because they have underestimated the level of effort required to successfully implement these radical changes and the level of resistance to change by employees and stakeholders.

To avoid this scenario, it is important that there is a compelling reason for change and a firm commitment by senior officials to support the initiative. The philosophy of 'think big, start small and scale fast' should be a central theme for re-engineering projects. A clear vision that is succinctly articulated conveys a focused sense of purpose to the organisation. Quick wins are necessary to create momentum, build credibility and demonstrate tangible progress.

4.6 Communications management

Change has two underpinning requirements: effective handling of the politics of change and careful attention to the management of change. Without the former, the change process will not survive as it will succumb to resistance; without the latter, it cannot be translated into results as successful management communication creates positive channels to support the change. At the heart of both requirements is a communications framework.

Building a robust communications network is important to deliver a consistent message, minimise the unknown or speculation, establish trust and confidence, maintain moral and motivation, share knowledge and gain feedback.

Communication needs to start from the top and should be frequent. People receive and interpret messages in different ways; therefore using multiple media ensures that messages are received. For a communications effort to be sincere and effective it requires effort, resources and tools on a sustained basis during the entire course of the implementation process.

Choosing the right communication tools and channels also depends on the status of the change process (Figure 4.4) – including newsletters and notices to build awareness, intranet and presentations to support understanding, focus groups and meetings to foster acceptance, and workshops and seminars to establish ownership and engagement.

4.7 Where GPR has brought results

4.7.1 Singapore

Singapore used GPR extensively during 2000–2006 to reinvent government and position Singapore as a global information communication hub, e-economy and e-society. During 2007, a survey was developed by Mr Albert Tan (Lecturer, Institute of Systems Science, National University of Singapore) and sent to private and public

Figure 4.4 Choosing the right communication tools and channels

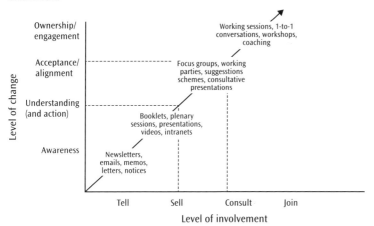

sector organisations. Forty-five per cent of respondents indicated that their GPR projects had achieved target benefits or exceeded them. Some examples of GPR projects are detailed below.

Box 4.2 The One-Stop Non-Stop (OSNS) Service

The aim is to bring Singapore's government services to the public at their convenience. Various government application systems are linked and deployed to minimise multiple form filling and multiple trips to different government departments. In addition, information kiosks are installed in public places – for example, in community centres, libraries, MRT (Mass Rapid Transit) stations and major bus interchanges – to enable public to access to government information easily, or for people to submit government application forms, pay government taxes, car park fees or fines, or to renew licences at places most convenient to them.

Box 4.3 Singapore's Public Services Infrastructure (PSi)

PSi is a central platform that government agencies can use to easily and efficiently build their own e-services. It offers common application services, such as payment gateways, data exchanges, authentication and security services, which help government agencies to generate their own online services, saving them the cost and time of developing or purchasing them independently.

Source: UNPAN 2003

Box 4.4 The Government Cloud (G-Cloud)

The central Government Cloud is the next-generation infrastructure, which will replace Singapore's current whole-of-government infrastructure (SHINE). It will provide central services, such as government web service exchange, and gateways to SingPass and e-payment services.

To further maximise cost savings to government, common services such as customer relationship management and web content management will be offered on the G-Cloud. This will enable standardisation and sharing of computing resources and applications at the whole-of-government level.

4.7.2 Malta

The Government of Malta applied GPR to bring its ministries in line with the requirements to enter into the European Union. As a result of their initiatives, the 2010 *e-Government Benchmarking* Report, which measured public sector performance in the deployment of e-government, showed Malta to be the best performing country in Europe by achieving 100 per cent in five of the six core indicator measures (online sophistication, full online availability, user experience for e-services, user experience for national portals, e-procurement visibility and e-procurement availability (MITC 2010). The government has launched an e-Procurement Gateway to improve its score in the final indicator.

4.7.3 India

Government agencies in India have made efforts to re-engineer public services to make them more efficient, available and less costly for citizens to use.

Box 4.5 Bhoomi: management of land records in Karnataka

Bhoomi was initiated in Karnataka, India, with the objective of re-engineering an age-old process of maintenance of land records. The old, manual system of land-record management hindered collection and analysis of data. Over time, inaccuracies crept into the system through improper management and deliberate manipulation and bribery by village accountants.

Twenty million land records were computerised and a network of Bhoomi record access points was set up in 177 locations, serving more than 6 million farmers. Farmers can now obtain computerised records at the click of a button or through touch-screen – and in a fraction of the previous time and cost. Apart from achieving the transparency, accountability and authenticity of data, there are other intangible benefits – such as arresting further distortion in data by creating a secure environment and creating equitable service to all on a first-come, first-served basis. See Rahman 2010.

Box 4.6 CARD: Andhra Pradesh

Similar to the Bhoomi project, the Computer-aided Administration of Registration Documentation (CARD) project was designed to make the registration of land deeds faster, more efficient, more reliable and consistent through computerisation, and to improve the citizen interface. The project was implemented in 214 locations in 15 months. It involved significant process re-engineering, involving detailed project management, capacity building (10% of total budget), outsourcing software development and changes to the Rules of Property Valuations and the Registration Act to improve transparency and efficiency. Registration can now take place in one hour instead of the previous 10 days.

Box 4.7 e-CheckPost, Gujarat

The Gujarat State Road Transport Department's computerised check post project has reduced corruption at Gujarat's borders and enhanced revenue earnings. The moment a truck enters Gujarat, its weight is recorded on a computer and all vehicle details, including the number plate, are photographed. This information is accessible at the control room in Ahmedabad, making it impossible for officials at the post to record a lower weight against a bribe.

The project was awarded gold in 2012 for the best government process re-engineering project in India. Strong political will (championed by the Government of Gujarat and the Transport Commissioner) as well as the efficient reconfiguration of the system, have been listed as key success points (UNPAN 2008).

Box 4.8 Integrated delivery of services: E-Biz India

The vision of E-Biz is to transform India's business environment. This is to be achieved by providing efficient, convenient, transparent and integrated electronic services to investors, industries and business sectors across all forms and procedures, approvals, clearances, permissions, reporting, filing, payments and compliances throughout the industry lifecycle. Central to what E-Biz looks to achieve is a radical shift in service delivery to business communities – from department-centric to customer-centric services. The initial stage of the project envisages the integrated delivery of 25 services provided by 14 central, provincial and local governments.

4.7.4 Lessons learned

There are several key lessons learned from the implementation of GPR in governments around the world. First, do not underestimate the effort required to manage and implement change initiatives. A compelling reason for change is critical in order to establish the impetus and will to undertake radical change. Visible and continuous support from senior management is also mandatory to drive change. Re-engineering involves risk and therefore perfection cannot be expected. To see it through, a 'stick-with-it' attitude must be taken – do not stop at early successes or problems. Finally, always remember the customer and look at processes from their perspective. The objective of re-engineering is to improve the cost, speed and quality of services that are provided to citizens; therefore re-engineering should create new systems that are customer-focused and add value for the customer.

4.8 GPR and governance

According to the United Nations Development Programme (undated), 'Good governance is, among other things, participatory, transparent and accountable. It is also effective and equitable. And it promotes the rule of law. Good governance ensures that political, social and economic priorities are based on broad consensus in society and that the voices of the poorest and the most vulnerable are heard in decision-making over the allocation of development resources'.

A key element in governance is how information is disseminated and used to hold governments to account for their actions, and how information could create the impetus for change. Since GPR is focused on citizens, it transforms the traditional citizens-to-government relationship where government provides inadequate information to protect vested interests.

Re-engineering forces bureaucrats to completely rethink the way business is conducted and react to the demands made by their constituents. Information could be provided with ease of access through a public-facing portal, and the veracity of the information could be confirmed through a variety of means – for instance, companies who were successful in procurement opportunities, and media reports on government performance. The ability of citizens and other stakeholders to assess government performance creates necessary tension and pressures that force government to be more open and accountable. Re-engineering also leverages modern technologies to create virtual pressure groups that cross geographical and social barriers with a singular focus to effect change or hold politicians to account for their actions.

References
eFarmDirect (2012), eFarmDirect, available at: www.efarmdirect.com/FAQ.php (accessed October 2012).

Hammer, M (1990), 'Reengineering work: Don't automate, obliterate', *Harvard Business Review*, Vol. 68 No. 4, 104–112.

Ming, A (2012), 'Government Process Re-engineering', *Commonwealth Ministers Reference Book 2012*, Henley Media Group, London.

Ministry for Infrastructure, Transport and Communications (MITC) (2010), *e-government benchmarking 2010*, MITC, Malta, available at: www.mita.gov.mt/MediaCenter/PDFs/1_eGovernmentBenchmarking_2010_highres.pdf (accessed October 2012).

Rahman, N (2010), *Governance Process Innovation for Improved Service Delivery*, India Governance, available at: http://indiagovernance.gov.in/files/GovernanceInnovation4PublicService.pdf (accessed October 2012).

United Nations Development Programme (undated), 'Good Governance – and Sustainable Human Development', UNDP, available at: http://mirror.undp.org/magnet/policy/chapter1.htm (accessed October 2012).

UN Public Administration Network (UNPAN) (2003), 'Factsheet of Public Services Infrastructure', MOF Singapore, available at: http://unpan1.un.org/intradoc/groups/public/documents/APCITY/UNPAN014669.pdf (accessed October 2012).

UNPAN (2008), *Computerised Interstate Check Posts of Gujurat State, India. A cost-benefit evaluation study*, Centre for Electronic Governance, UNPAN, available at: http://unpan1.un.org/intradoc/groups/public/documents/Other/UNPAN022731.pdf (accessed October 2012).

Chapter 5

e-Governance Implementation

David Spiteri Gingell

The previous chapters have established that the best route to the attainment of e-government is through the design of a holistic strategy that seeks to transform government, and subsequently transform a country, into an information society or information economy.

It has also been explained that the design of the strategic process to achieve such a transformation demands that the strategy is designed over a generational horizon. Transformation will not happen overnight. It will require various stages of maturity – with each level of maturity leading to subsequent stages of development until these too reach a level of maturity.

Small states have to face unique challenges, which will impact the tempo and pace of the implementation process. This, however, does not mean that e-government is not attainable. It is important to underline that a considerable number of the constituent parts to achieve e-government do not carry major costs. Moreover, the economics of ICT have changed rendering the cost of technology cheaper and more affordable. Furthermore, the technology itself has changed. Mobile telephony has now proved that it is a strong enabler for the attainment of e-government, as invariably it is less expensive to implement than dark fibre infrastructure, more affordable to citizens and overcomes the challenge of distance.

An approach to the attainment of e-government should therefore be designed to be multi-pronged from the outset of the implementation process, particularly with regards to the establishment of the underlying soft and hard infrastructure necessary for its successful implementation.

5.1 Legislative, regulatory and policy components

5.1.1 E-commerce legislation

A cyber-legislative framework should, to the extent possible, precede the implementation of an e-government strategy in order to ensure legal effect, confidence and trust, and protection against misuse and abuse. The launch and implementation of an e-government strategy can be critically undermined, and potentially result in political embarrassment, in the event that an appropriate cyber-legislative framework is not in place. Without e-commerce legislation, electronic transactions will have no legal validity or effect.

The absence of legal validity and effect will create jurisprudence and legal issues. Thus, e-commerce legislation must be in place, ideally prior to the initiation of e-services.

Electronic commerce legislation can be designed to act as a vehicle to intensify the uptake of e-government interaction – between government institutions and citizens as well as businesses – by rendering it mandatory for a person to interact electronically with any government entity where any law of the country requires or permits a person to: (i) give information in writing; (ii) provide a signature; (iii) produce a document; and/or (iv) record information. An electronic commerce and transactions law and regulatory framework should address a number of principles. These include:

- the importance of a secure legal basis for electronic communications, contracts, signatures and transactions so as to:

  - encourage economic activity; and

  - allow for the provision of government services over electronic communications media.

- protection of both the consumer and the service provider;

- the need to set minimum rules for providers of 'information society services', though avoiding barriers to entry into this business; and

- the international rules relating to e-commerce.

Box 5.1 Good examples of e-commerce legislation

The United Nations Commission on International Trade Law (UNCITRAL) Model Law on E-Commerce of 1996 (UN 1999) provides an excellent basis to draft an e-commerce and transactions act. Other good models which have withstood the test of time are:

- The Maltese Electronic Commerce Act

- The Australian e-Commerce and Transactions Act

- The Irish Electronic Commerce Act

See: UNICITRAL 1999; Government of Malta 2002; Australian Government 1999; Office of the Attorney General 2000

The principles to be applied in drawing up an e-commerce legislative and regulatory framework include:

- The regulatory framework must be flexible enough to keep up with advances in technology.

- The regulatory framework should observe the principles of self-regulation and subsidiarity, and should refrain from adopting mandatory authorisation systems for signature certification of service providers, although voluntary accreditation schemes could prove useful.

- As electronic signatures must be legally recognised, basic requirements and responsibilities for qualified certificates must be specified.

- Electronic signatures that are based on a qualified certificate issued by a signature certification service provider and which fulfil the requirements established, should be mandatorily recognised as satisfying the legal requirement of a hand-written signature. They should be admissible as evidence in legal proceedings in the same manner as hand-written signatures.

- Electronic signatures used within closed groups, for example where contractual relationships already exist, should not automatically fall within the scope of a legislation as contractual freedom should prevail in such a context.

- The regulatory framework should ensure legal recognition – in particular across borders – of electronic signatures and of certification services. This involves clarifying the essential requirements for signature certification service providers, including their liability.

- The service provider must be able to transmit the data concerning the identity of a user adopting a pseudonym to the public authorities upon request, with the prior consent of the person in question.

- Commercial communications (advertising, direct marketing etc.) – which are embraced by electronic communications – are perceived to constitute an integral part of most electronic commerce services. Such clarifications should be issued on the basis of regulations.

- Electronic commerce will not develop fully if concluding online contracts is hampered by certain requirements that are not adapted to the online environment. Thus an e-commerce legislative and regulatory framework should embrace electronic documents, which include contracts. The legislative framework should propose parameters of when a document is valid, which include time and place of receipt, time of dispatch and storage.

- Liability of intermediary service providers should be planned for, such as:

  - the mere transmission of information over their communications network;

  - temporary storage of information in their network (caching); or

  - storage of information (hosting).

5.1.2 Data protection and privacy legislation

The second component is data protection and privacy legislation, which will secure the rules of how government entities are to employ 'personal data'. The presence of data protection legislation will increase the level of trust and confidence in the use and take-up of e-services.

There are, essentially, three models of data protection legislation design. One is the EU legislative model, the parameters of which are established by Directive 95/46/EC of the European Parliament and of the Council of 24 October 1995, on the protection of individuals with regard to the processing of personal data and on the free movement of such data (EU 1995). The EU legislative model provides for the heavy regulated use of data, and is basically premised on the philosophy that use of data may be abused and hence a tight regulatory regime is necessary to mitigate for such abuse. However, the directive was drawn up before the widespread use of the internet, and the arising business models, including e-government, which this spawned. During the late-1990s and the early-2000s, considerable debate took place between some member states and the European Commission on the need to effect a lighter regime based on the principle of good and reasonable use, as it was otherwise believed that the benefits that could accrue from the implementation of an e-government business model would be constrained.

The *Swedish Personal Data Act* (Government of Sweden 1998) is a good example to follow in the event that a country is seeking to introduce a strong regulatory regime for data protection legislation with a minimalist bias.

A second model is the design of legislation on the principle of good and reasonable use stated above. In essence this model establishes that all use of data is permissible unless otherwise restricted or governed by ad hoc legislation. This model reflects the degree and maturity of the trust that citizens hold in government and other institutions.

A third model combines data protection principles with freedom of information. Few countries have followed this particular design. In part this is because data protection is directed towards safeguarding the individual's right to privacy, while freedom of information is directed towards entrenching open government and placing governing institutions under direct public scrutiny and accountability for decisions taken.

The appropriate model that a country should adopt to design its data protection legislation should balance, on the one hand, the political culture of the polity and the level of trust and confidence by citizens in the governing institutions with, on the other hand, the degree of information sharing flexibility it seeks to achieve to optimise the opportunities of e-government and the cyber-world, as well as the cost it is ready to pay and impose on business, for a highly regulated regime.

The provisions in the Swedish legislation with regards to the *Competent Authority* are sparsely defined. The drafters of data protection legislation may consider that allowing such discretion in the interpretation of the said powers to the Competent Authority could potentially undermine the spirit that the legislation seeks to achieve; this is given that the role of the Competent Authority could be dependent on the person holding the office of the said Authority. The drafters may argue that such a broad degree of discretion would not be in the nation's best interests, as a Supervisory Authority that adopts a 'purist' approach could arguably result in over-regulation. This in turn could lead to increasingly heavy administration regulation costs, as well as the restriction of the use of data for virtual e-government services. The drafters, therefore, may conclude that it is important that the responsibilities of the Competent Authority are specified in detail within the legislation – thereby minimising to the extent possible the level of administrative discretion. In this regard, the drafters of the legislation may conclude that the definition of the powers of the Competent Authority as specified in the *Italian Personal Data Protection Code* is a good model to follow (see: www. dataprotection.it/codice_privacy_english.htm).

5.1.3 Computer misuse legislation

In terms of establishing the legislative, regulatory and policy instruments necessary for the successful implementation of e-government, the third component is computer misuse legislation. The cyber-world, and thus e-government, gives rise to new crimes that are not governed by traditional criminal legislation. The absence of computer misuse legislation will leave a government and citizens vulnerable to e-crimes as they occur.

In designing computer misuse legislation, the following good practices and principles should be taken into consideration:

- The legislation should be technologically neutral, both in terms of the threats it seeks to provide safeguards against, as well in terms of the definition of what constitutes technology. As has been experienced over the past ten years, threats evolve continuously and as rapidly, indeed if not more so, as technology innovation. Seeking to identify types of threats and technologies will increase the risk for continuous amendments to legislation, as new threats and technologies emerge. This will constrain the effectiveness of the legislation and will render its administration cumbersome at best.

- One of the key difficulties with regards to prosecuting a person in relation to a computer crime is that of proving the person's intent to actually commit a crime. Too often, legal actions against computer crime offences fail as a result of this. A potential safeguard against this scenario is to design computer misuse legislation in such a manner that the kernel determining whether a person is guilty of an offence stems from the fact that the person acted 'without authorisation' when the act was carried out. Legislation can be furthered strengthened if the burden of proof to show that a person has acted with/without authorisation is placed on the person accused of the offence. This is the approach that Malta took with regard to its computer misuse provisions.

- However, adopting such an approach demands that the government entity responsible for ICT, or in a decentralised environment each entity that has responsibility for ICT resources, has to adopt a rigorous approach to security policy design and its dissemination. This will ensure, for example, that access to any ICT resources carries a notification that informs users that such access is legal only if the person seeking it is authorised to do so. Access rights and privileges, for example, should be formalised so that an accountability trail is in place. This safeguards persons who have been assigned authorisation and establishes with absolute clarity those who have not been provided with authorisation. It is important to note that the absence of formal security policies and measures would render the task of proving in a court of law that an individual acted without authorisation difficult for the government entity concerned.

It is pertinent to underline that many organisations form protection strategies by focusing solely on infrastructure weaknesses; they fail to establish the effect on their most important information assets. This leads to a gap between an organisations' operational and information technology (IT) requirements, placing the assets at risk. Approaches to information security risk management may be incomplete: they could fail to include all components of risk (assets, threats and vulnerabilities). Thus the planning and implementation of comprehensive and robust information security architecture is of paramount importance in the cyber-world – which e-government defaults into.

Box 5.2 Examples of methodologies relating to information security management

Risk management assessment – OCTAVE

The Operationally Critical Threat, Asset and Vulnerability Evaluation SM (OCTAVE[SM]) is an approach to information security risk evaluations that is comprehensive, systematic, context-driven and self-directed. The approach is embodied in a set of criteria that define the essential elements of an asset-driven information security risk evaluation. The OCTAVE criteria require the evaluation to be led and performed by a small, interdisciplinary analysis team of the organisation's business and IT personnel. Team members work together to make decisions based on risks to critical information assets. Finally, the OCTAVE criteria require catalogues of information to measure organisational practices, analyse threats and build protection strategies. These catalogues are: (i) catalogue of practices – a collection of good strategic and operational security practices; (ii) generic threat profile – a collection of major sources of threats; and (iii) catalogue of vulnerabilities – a collection of vulnerabilities based on platform and application.

(Continued)

Box 5.2 Examples of methodologies relating to information security management (cont.)

OCTAVE-S was developed in response to the needs of smaller organisations (of around 100 people or less). It meets the same criteria as the OCTAVE method, but is adapted to the more limited means and unique constraints of small organisations. OCTAVE-S uses a more streamlined process and different worksheets, but it produces the same type of results. Before you use OCTAVE-S, consider the two primary differences in this version of OCTAVE: (i) OCTAVE-S requires a small team of three to five people who understand the breadth and depth of the company; and (ii) OCTAVE-S includes only a limited exploration of the computing infrastructure. Small companies frequently outsource their IT completely and do not have the ability to run or interpret the results of vulnerability tools.

Information security architecture methodology – SABSA

The Sherwood Applied Business Security Architecture (SABSA) is a model and a methodology for developing risk-driven enterprise information security architectures, and for delivering security infrastructure solutions that support critical business initiatives. The primary characteristic of the SABSA model is that everything must be derived from an analysis of the business requirements for security, especially those in which security has an enabling function through which new business opportunities can be developed and exploited.

The process analyses the business requirements at the outset, and creates a chain of traceability through the strategy and concept, design, implementation and ongoing 'manage and measure' phases of the lifecycle to ensure that the business mandate is preserved. Framework tools created from practical experience further support the whole methodology. The model is layered, with the top layer being the business requirements definition stage. At each lower layer a new level of abstraction and detail is developed, going through the definition of the conceptual architecture, logical services architecture, physical infrastructure architecture and finally at the lowest layer, the selection of technologies and products (component architecture).

The SABSA model itself is generic and can be the starting point for any organisation. However, by going through the process of analysis and decision-making implied by its structure, it becomes specific to the enterprise and is finally highly customised to a unique business model. It becomes in reality the enterprise security architecture, and it is central to the success of a strategic programme of information security management within the organisation.

Information security governance – COBIT

Control Objectives for Information and related Technology (COBIT®) provides good practices across a domain and process framework, and presents activities in a

> **Box 5.2 Examples of methodologies relating to information security management (cont.)**
>
> manageable and logical structure. COBIT's good practices represent the consensus of experts. They are more strongly focused on control, and less on execution. These practices help optimise IT-enabled investments, ensure service delivery and provide a measure against which to judge when things do go wrong. The business orientation of COBIT consists of linking business goals to IT goals, providing metrics and maturity models to measure their achievement, and identifying the associated responsibilities of business and IT process owners. The process focus of COBIT is illustrated by a process model that subdivides IT into 4 domains and 34 processes in line with the responsibility areas of plan, build, run and monitor, providing an end-to-end view of IT. Enterprise architecture concepts help identify the resources essential for process success, i.e., applications, information, infrastructure and people.
>
> COBIT 5, the latest edition of ISACA's globally accepted framework, was set to consolidate and integrate the COBIT 4.1, Val IT 2.0 and Risk IT frameworks and also to draw significantly from the Business Model for Information Security (BMIS) and Information Technology Assurance Framework ITAF (ISACA 2013). At the time of writing, it was perceived that COBIT 5 would be a major strategic improvement providing the next generation of Information Systems Audit and Control Association ISACA's guidance on the enterprise governance of IT. Building on more than 15 years of practical usage and application of COBIT by many enterprises and users from the business, IT, security and assurance communities, COBIT 5 was to be designed to meet the current needs of stakeholders and align with the most up-to-date thinking in enterprise governance and IT management techniques.

5.1.4 Liberalisation of the telecommunications sector

The uptake of internet connectivity by households is directly correlated to the cost – be that through dial-up or broadband connectivity. The cost of access to internet connectivity is, in turn, directly correlated to the liberalisation of the telecommunication process and the state of its maturity. Given this strong correlation, a process of telecommunications liberalisation is one of the first sectoral reforms that will support the implementation of an e-government strategy.

International experience shows that the liberalisation of a country's telecommunications sector results in a lowering, through competition, of user fees to access internet and mobile services. The uptake of e-government can only take place if citizens and entrepreneurs have access to the technology and can afford accessibility to the technology. An environment where technological choice is limited and access to technology is not affordable will result in the failure of the e-government strategy.

Figure 5.1 Telecommunications reform in Botswana: a policy model

Since the mid-1990s, Botswana has pursued a policy of telecommunications liberalisation. This process is considered to be a model worthy of emulation. The participation and protection of domestic telecommunication users, transparency in decision-making, the creation of an independent regulatory agency and the introduction of competition in the form of private mobile phone providers are among those features that are recommended for replication.

Botswana telecommunications liberalisation process:

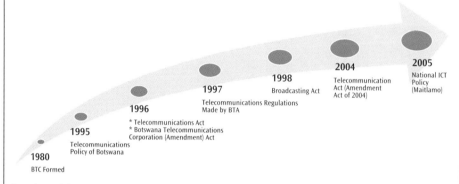

Functions of the Botswana Telecommunications Authority:

(1) The Authority shall supervise and promote the provision of efficient telecommunication services in Botswana.

(2) Without derogating from the generality of the provision of Subsection (1), the Authority shall –

    (a) take all reasonable steps to promote the provision, throughout Botswana, of such telecommunication services, as will satisfy all reasonable demands for them including emergency services, public call box services and directory information services;

    (b) promote the interests of consumers, purchasers and other users of telecommunication services in respect of the prices charged for, and the quality and variety of, such services and equipment or terminal equipment supplied for the purposes of such services; and

    (c) promote and maintain competition among persons engaged in commercial activities for, or in connection with, the provision of telecommunication services, and promote efficiency and economy on the part of persons so engaged.

(3) The Authority shall have, and may exercise and perform, such other powers and functions as may be conferred on it by, or under this or any other Act.

(4) The Board may, in writing, delegate any of the powers and functions of the Authority to the Chief Executive or any other officer of the Authority.

(5) The Minister may, after consultation with the Board, give the Board directions of a general or specific nature regarding the exercise of its powers and the performance of its functions, which directions shall not be inconsistent with this Act or with the contractual or other legal obligations of the Authority, and the Authority shall give effect to any such directions.

(6) Subject to the provisions of Subsection (5), the Authority shall not be subject to the direction of any other person or authority in the exercise of its functions under Parts V, VI, VII and VIII of this Act (see: www.elaws.gov.bw/pr_export.php?id=157).

An immediate first step is the drafting of the enabling act for the setting up of a communications regulator. The legislation should be principle-based and should focus on the roles and responsibilities of the regulatory authority. Legal frameworks for the various telecommunications sectors – fixed telephony, mobile, internet and VoIP (Voice over Internet Protocol) spectrum etc. – should be introduced as subsidiary legislation.

The independence of national regulatory agencies is one of the fundamental underpinnings of successful liberalisation and in achieving competition. Such independence creates the conditions that: are conducive to investment; incentivise new market entrants with the prospect of a level playing field; achieve a stable regulatory landscape; and achieve one that is not susceptible to political whim. In order to foster independence, several formal safeguards have been employed to achieve such a balance (infoDev and ITU 2012). These include:

- Providing the regulator with a distinct statutory authority, free of ministerial control.

- Prescribing well-defined professional criteria for appointments.

- Involving both the executive and the legislative branches of government in the appointment process.

- Appointing regulators (the director general or board/commission members) for a fixed period of time and prohibiting their removal (subject to formal review), except for clearly defined due cause.

- Where a collegiate (board/commission) structure has been chosen, staggering the terms of members so that they can be replaced only gradually by each successive government.

- Providing the agency with a reliable and adequate source of funding. Ideally, charges for specific services or levies on the sector can be used to fund the regulator to insulate it from political interference through the budget process.

- Exempting the regulator from civil service salary limits to attract and retain the best-qualified staff and to ensure adequate good governance incentives.

- Prohibiting the executive from overturning the agency's decisions, except through carefully designed channels – such as new legislation or appeals to the courts based on existing law.

However, sector-specific regulatory expertise is an uncommon commodity at the best of times, and understandably more so in a smaller country. Therefore, government should consider extending a telecommunications regulator's jurisdiction to address sector competition either concurrently, i.e. the two agencies collaborating, or exclusively for the telecommunications regulator to adjudicate on competition matters within its jurisdictional sectors.

Policy mechanisms for both delivering and financing the desired level of service include market-based reforms, mandatory service obligations, leveraging new technologies (e.g. mobile devices), leveraging new business practices (e.g. pre-paid cards), cross-subsidies, access deficit charges and public–private partnerships. Of these, the most successful have been the market-based reforms associated with the liberalisation of the mobile sector, supported by a stable regulatory environment and the subsequent exponential growth in customers in developing countries.

The ICT Regulation Toolkit developed by infoDev in conjunction with ITU is a rich resource for capacity building and could serve as a vital reference in the design of a telecommunications liberalisation strategy (Box 5.3).

Box 5.3 ICT Regulation Toolkit

The toolkit is intended to assist regulators with the design of effective and enabling regulatory frameworks to harness the latest technological and market advances. Its most prevalent themes are the impact of changing technology, the role of competition and the regulatory implications of the transition from traditional telephony to next generation networks. The toolkit incorporates the following modules:

- Regulating the Telecommunications Sector: Overview

- Competition and Price Regulation

- Authorisation of Telecommunications Services

- Universal Access and Services

- Radio Spectrum Management – Legal and Institutional Framework

- New Technologies and Impact on Regulation

Source: infoDev and ITU 2012

5.2 Development of ICT architecture and standards

5.2.1 The provision of electronic mail and internet access to government employees

One immediate first step, if not already achieved, is to provide internet access and an electronic mail (email) account to every employee within a government entity. This will have two pervasive impacts. First, particularly if this is followed by a policy decision that mandates that all communication between entities is to be carried out by electronic mail and documents, it will instil an e-culture among public officers and government employees. A consequential ripple effect is that such a step will also facilitate communications between government entities and external constituents.

Second, given that in small and island states the government is normally the largest employer, the provision of electronic communications and internet access translates into a good step in engendering an information society, as a large proportion of persons in employment would be exposed to ICT.

Such an approach may have a greater impact should the diffusion of ICT within households still be limited. In such a situation, access to electronic communications and the internet from the office or terminals for public officers who are not necessarily deskbound (police officers, teachers, nurses) will initially be the primary gateway to the e-world. The experience of Malta has shown that the adoption of this approach, together with steps taken to increase affordability of computer hardware and internet access would, within a relatively short time, nudge such employees to invest in home connectivity as they recognise the power of the internet in terms of knowledge, information and other opportunities.

5.2.2 Enterprise architecture
The development of the e-government platform should be preceded by an enterprise architecture. An enterprise architecture enables the entity assigned responsibility for implementation to establish a road-map that will allow for optimal performance of the e-government value chain within an efficient, scalable, modular, coherent and interoperable underlying ICT framework.

Simply stated, enterprise architectures are blueprints for systematically and completely defining the current ICT (baseline) or desired (target) environment. Enterprise architectures are, therefore, essential for evolving information systems and developing new systems that optimise their mission value – in this case, a seamless e-government value chain. If defined, maintained and implemented effectively, such institutional blueprints assist in optimising the interdependencies and interrelationships along the e-government value chain and the business operations of the myriad government entities that will be interlocked to it and the underlying ICT framework (US Government 2001).

In general, the essential reasons for developing an enterprise architecture include:

(i)   alignment – that is, ensuring that the reality of the implemented enterprise is aligned with management's intent;

(ii) integration – that is, ensuring that the business rules are consistent across the organisation, that the data and its use are immutable, interfaces and information flow are standardised, and the connectivity and interoperability are managed across the enterprise;

(iii) change – that is, facilitating and managing change to any aspect of the enterprise;

(iv) time-to-market – that is, reducing systems development, applications generation, modernisation timeframes and resource requirements; and convergence – that is, striving towards a standard ICT product portfolio (US Government 2001).

There is no single methodology on how an enterprise architecture process should be performed. It is argued that the enterprise architecture process should be fitted to the individual organisation. In fact there are various enterprise architecture frameworks that can be adopted by an organisation – such as the Zachman Enterprise Architecture Framework, the Open Group Architecture Framework (TOGAF) and Service Oriented Architecture (SOA) (see Annex 5.1).

5.2.3 Design of interoperability standards

Unless a government introduces interoperability standards to be adopted by all agencies within the government at the outset, then the e-government strategy will be susceptible to failure. E-government means that government entities need to network with one another, with data seamlessly exchanged between one agency and the others to allow e-services to take effect.

An e-government interoperability framework (e-GIF) is a set of policies, technical standards and guidelines. It covers ways to achieve interoperability of public sector data and information resources, information and communications technology (ICT) and electronic business processes. It enables any agency to join its information, ICT or processes with those of any other agency using a predetermined framework based on 'open' (i.e. non-proprietary) international standards. An e-GIF performs the same function in e-government as the road/highway code does on the roads. Driving would be excessively costly, inefficient and ineffective if road rules had to be agreed each time one vehicle encountered another.

From a technical standpoint, e-government interoperability is achieved when the coherent, electronic exchange of information and services between systems takes place. E-government interoperability relates specifically to the electronic systems that support business processes between agencies, government and people, and government and business.

This does not mean a central agency simply dictating common systems and processes. Interoperability can be achieved by applying a framework of policies, standards and guidelines that leave decisions about specific hardware and software solutions open for individual agencies, or clusters of agencies, to resolve.

An e-GIF will:

• help government agencies to work more easily together electronically;

• make systems, knowledge and experience re-usable from one agency to another;

• reduce the effort needed to deal with government online by encouraging consistency of approach; and

- reduce reliance on tapes and disks to exchange data, as these carry their own security issues and are not scalable for the level of interoperability many services will need in future (New Zealand State Services Commission 2008).

Moreover, the internet and the value it can deliver to government and people, relies on an agreed, standards-based approach. By using the same standards-based approach, agencies support the infrastructure of technologies that they increasingly rely on to deliver services and conduct the business of government. Adopting common standards also helps governments in various jurisdictions to interoperate. This becomes important when dealing with matters that can only be handled on a regional or global basis.

The New Zealand e-Government Interoperability Framework is a good practice model to follow (New Zealand State Services Commission 2008). (For further details on interoperability standards, see Annex 5.2).

Box 5.4   Transition to an e-government interoperability framework: New Zealand

The adoption of the e-GIF must allow for a sensible transition. Recognising this, the New Zealand Cabinet agreed on 13 June 2002 that current information systems, software applications and electronic data/information resources did not need to comply immediately with the e-GIF. However, any new information system, software application and electronic data/information resource (or current instances of these being redeveloped or replaced), along with systems for interfacing with these, must comply with the e-GIF. The only exceptions are:

- if developers are certain that interoperability will never be a requirement; or

- if the current version of the e-GIF does not, and could not, include policies, standards or guidelines concerning the technologies the agency needs (not wants) to employ.

If an agency has one of these exceptional instances, it needs to consider the customer perspective. Although the agency system may have been developed to operate in isolation, New Zealanders may one day need it, transparently or otherwise, to work with other services from other agencies. Is it certain that the new system, application or resource will never need to support or interact with any new, enhanced or replacement system, application, interface, service, process or resource? Experience shows that in most cases, the e-GIF will apply.

The absence of an interoperability framework will most likely result in a situation where agencies introduce e-services independently of one another. The likelihood is that, in striving to introduce their respective e-services, they will adopt their own sets of standards. In the event that this happens, then interoperability would require expensive retrofitting to be achieved. This is an unnecessary and unwarranted financial cost that should be avoided.

5.2.4 Development of a government central portal

An unco-ordinated approach towards the introduction of websites across government entities may complement difficulties in tracking down the right organisation for the right services that prevails today with regard to traditional service delivery. The interface between the public and the e-government world must be seamless to the greatest extent possible by establishing a clear, simple, and transparent gateway for the user. The best way to achieve this is to design a central portal, owned by the entity responsible for e-government initiatives, which provides the user with electronic access to both entities and services. Services can be shown individually or designed around a cluster to facilitate the search for the appropriate service. One particular methodology is to design the clusters around a person's life journey: health; education; employment; leisure; family affairs etc.

The immediate visible impact in terms of the scale of activity being adopted by the government in rendering basic e-services available to the polity is considerable. Initially, such an approach will only meet the first phase of the e-government pathway, discussed in Chapter 1, in that it will provide information to the public and establish an electronic channel between the public and with each and every entity within government.

Too often, focus is directed towards launching a website as against managing the website once it is launched. Too often, websites remain static and electronic communication channelled through them fails to receive the same level of attention as conventional mail communication. A static website is a strong negative signal of the fact that an e-culture has not taken root within the organisation responsible for it. Static websites can only become dynamic if they are managed.

Furthermore, the e-government platform should, from the outset, ensure that no part of society is marginalised in the e-environment as a result of access being hindered due to language barriers. Thus, all e-services should be designed on a bi- or multi-language platform to secure full accessibility.

5.2.5 Transactions and e-services

In tandem with the introduction of a government website, each government entity should review its forms and place each form for electronic access through the website. This provides an excellent channel for the end user to be able to interact electronically with the government entity without the need to physically obtain the forms from the relevant organisation.

The design implementation of important e-government sub projects that can be carried out in the immediate and short term track of e-government activities that includes 'throw away' solutions provides an excellent way forward in balancing, on the one hand, the time required to introduce a robust e-government platform and, on the other, the need to mobilise fast to create a sustainable momentum and credibility in the initiative.

Transactional e-services are the trigger for an electronic service without any physical intervention. The short-term track should provide a series of transactional solutions. It is these solutions that will demonstrate the true revolution of e-government. In adopting transactional e-services in the short-term track, there should be upfront recognition that to a large extent this will be a 'throw away' investment.

In identifying transactional short-term e-services for the short-term track, the following considerations should be taken into account:

- Identification of existing back-end applications that with investment of a level of effort can allow for web-enabled services – either in terms of adding a front-end or by appropriate modification.

- Identification of payment-based transaction services that can be designed through a temporary e-payment services provider.

- Identification of service-related applications that impact a wide cross-section of audiences, as against sectoral-based audiences in so far as this is possible.

- Identification of transactional e-services that are of minimum risk. It is pertinent to underline that an over-ambitious service that has a high level of risk may result in a potential fall-out, which could jeopardise the entire e-government strategy if it goes wrong.

In the long-term, the e-government platform should be:

- Able to cope with a variety of channels.

- Capable of providing access to all government back-end services from all delivery channels.

- Structured to accommodate different back-office requirements.

- Based on proven, widely available and used technology.

- Scalable to accommodate growing and changing usage requirements with cheap incremental increases in size.

- Equipped to handle digital authorisation.

- Capable of handling unpredictable volumes of traffic.

- Capable of handling an m-government gateway.

- Capable of handling an e-payment gateway.

The e-government platform should be flexible, scalable and modular, based on a three-tier architecture designed to integrate new delivery channels and add new e-services with minimal additional investment (Figure 5.2).

A three-tier architecture should be used to insulate the access channels from the complexity of the government back office, with web technology providing the portal or gateway between the channels and the individual service requested. The key concept of the three-tier architecture is the use of middleware technology to provide a brokerage capability. The middleware will link components to allow them to interact without the need to have knowledge of the other component's location, hardware platform or implementation technology.

5.2.6 The need for redundancy and consolidation[1]

Thus, the e-government platform must be designed around full redundancy (that is the provision of additional or duplicate aspects of equipment that will function in case an operating part of system fails) architecture at, at least, three end points. First, a country should ensure that its telecommunications provider/s, either within a monopolistic or liberalised environment, have in place two different entry points from two different international service providers. This will ensure that, in the event that one of the entry points suffers damage – for example an underwater cable being torn by a trawler – connectivity will continue to be provided through the second entry route.

Second, the country should ensure that local connectivity from the international connectivity gateway(s) to the data centre wherein the e-government technology infrastructure is sited, accesses the location from two different end points, and ideally from two different service providers.

Third, the economics of today's information technology have changed. The cost of technology has fallen, while the costs of licences and skilled labour have increased. Thus, the economics of information technology render a centralised and consolidated IT data centre cost effective, as the total cost of ownership is much cheaper than running a fragmented data centre environment in which centres are set up in key ministries and departments.

Data centres have ancillary costs – air-conditioning equipment, back-up generators, fire systems, monitoring tools etc. – which if replicated in every data centre created, will render the cost of operations prohibitive. Moreover, a fragmented data centre approach will increase the investment required considerably to ensure redundancy and, therefore, continuity of service in the event of planned or unplanned downtime.

Thus, the actual e-government platform should be fully redundant and designed on an 'Active–Active' basis, so that downtime on one particular part of the technology would allow the other redundant part to secure continued service provision without providing any denial of service outage.

Figure 5.2 Conceptual model of a three-tier e-government architecture

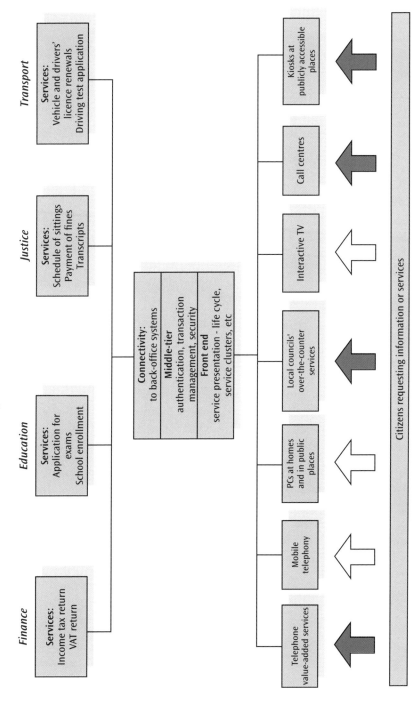

5.3 ICT infrastructure

The level of existing infrastructure also affects a country's ability to enable users to connect to the internet. The procurement and laying of dark fibre is expensive, although new technologies such as optical fibre have reduced the cost of laying fibre over short distances. Invariably, internet users are more likely to start taking root within urban communities.

Access to the internet can also be provided through satellites, particularly low earth orbit or geostationary satellites. Nevertheless, depending on the regions, different types of satellite systems have a wide range of different features and technical limitations, which can greatly affect usefulness and performance in specific applications.

5.3.1 Kiosks

In the early stages of the e-government implementation process, particularly while the telecommunication liberalisation process is in transition, the price to internet access will act as a hurdle for particular cohorts of the population to access e-services. This can be mitigated by low-cost delivery measures. These include:

- the establishment of internet kiosks in popular sites such as supermarkets, squares etc.;

- the establishment of internet kiosks in rural communities; and

- the placement of computer terminals with full internet access in town, village and rural schools and libraries.

In adopting such low-cost delivery measures, the government entity responsible for e-government implementation should seek strategic partnerships with private industry and telecommunications transport providers to finance, in part or in whole, the hardware and the cost of connectivity.

Experience shows that the introduction of such internet kiosks during the early stages of the implementation of e-government is a strategic action given that, at this stage of the implementation, access to and affordability of the internet may limit the up-take of e-government. Thus, the presence of internet kiosks at the stage when the implementation of the e-government strategy may be at its most vulnerable, may act as valuable channel in enabling access and in nurturing an information society.

Box 5.5   Setting up a multi-facility centre at a weekly marketplace in India

In its efforts to test its method for bringing ICTs to remote communities, Satpura Integrated Rural Development Institution (SIRDI) established a multi-facility centre at a weekly marketplace in Sawalmendha. Thousands of people from the surrounding 68 villages visit the market every week to purchase essential products and conduct routine work. SIRDI set up similar centres in Taluka Town, Bhainsdehi and the district town of Betul, and established a communication network between these villages and Sawalmendha.

The project addressed both technical and social issues. From a technical perspective, the main issues were to test how ICTs can be made to work in remote areas with limited infrastructure. Computers and other instruments were tested in harsh conditions and did not break down. Telephone lines were unreliable, however, and it took several months to activate the internet connection. In addition, the power supply in the state of Madhya Pradesh was limited. Electricity was available between four and eight hours per day, which was insufficient to charge the batteries of the uninterrupted power supply (UPS) and inverters. Hence, the generator backup planned as part of the project proved useful.

From a social perspective, the project sought to test whether weekly markets can provide a 'door-step' for access to ICTs, to assess the impact of the use of ICTs on tribal communities and understand the social and psychological factors that influence use or non-use of ICTs. The project noted that because of the beneficiaries' low literacy rate and general lack of awareness about ICTs, the community could not really benefit on a large scale during the short project period. It was also noted that response from villages was much healthier in those villages where SIRDI had already been working, and where social workers were already based. During the later stages of the project, local youth started taking interest in the activities of the centre and in learning internet technology skills. The percentage of requests for help submitted by women remained consistent throughout the project period at about 35 per cent.

5.3.2 National internet exchange

An administration should also consider creating a national internet exchange (NIE), particularly in the early stages of the development of the information society, in order to eliminate the situation where local traffic traverses costly international links and where one of the gateway providers may end up having a monopoly on the international gateway and internet exchange. If such a situation arises, connectivity to the internet will be expensive due to the relatively high costs of international data circuits.

The lack of a local interconnection scheme will mean that an email sent from one subscriber in the country to another will have to traverse through such costly links.

Moreover, it is also highly likely that the bandwidth on these international lines will be heavily over-subscribed, since such bandwidths are expensive and may be over-utilised. This in turn will result in poor and slow performance to access local sites – including the e-government platform.

The creation of a NIE provides a designated central exchange point, which prevents local traffic having to traverse costly international links. A national exchange independent of any gateway operator would also benefit from complete autonomy. Otherwise the situation may arise, with the advent of multiple international data gateway operators as the telecommunications sector matures, where one of the gateway providers is also responsible for managing an internet exchange.

5.3.3 Call centre provision of e-services

An e-government strategy that bases its delivery channels uniquely on the internet may discriminate against cohorts of the population who are not technology savvy and/or cannot afford or do not have access to technology. Nonetheless, most small and island states have a large penetration of fixed-line telephony. Although fixed-line technology as a delivery channel for e-services is often forgotten or introduced as an afterthought, it constitutes a highly effective way for the provision of e-services.

There are two ways in which an e-service can be provided through a fixed-line delivery channel. The first is where the user interacts with a call centre for the activation of an e-service transaction. In essence, the user contacts a call centre and, following identification, the call centre will activate the particular e-service transaction. In this case, a human 'air bubble' interface is created where the call centre agent acts as an intermediary on behalf of the user. The second is where the user interacts with a voice automated e-service transaction delivery channel, which is activated following user identification through a fixed-line call.

5.3.4 M-government

Moreover, the application of m-government – that is, the provision of e-services through mobile telephony – can be an extremely effective way to roll out e-government. This is particularly the case with 'push down' e-services, whereby a citizen may require a service without the need to transact back with the government agency service provider.

For example, m-services can be quickly introduced for the dissemination of information relating to weather changes in zones that may susceptible to quick climatic changes, the provision of weather forecasts to farmers in rural villages, the provision of health education etc.

M-government should be a strategic component in the design and implementation of an e-government platform, as it is far more cost effective to deploy than fixed telephone lines or fibre. This is particularly the case in countries where core infrastructure is limited to the capital city and large towns, because the penetration of mobile telephony is far more likely to be universal than internet connectivity. M-government increases the tempo of e-/m-services interaction uptake and the attainment of an information society. M-government is explored further in the following chapter.

5.4 Conclusion

The implementation of e-government strategies will take time. Laws take time to draft and the process leading up to the liberalisation of telecommunications infrastructure is complex, taking years before the full effects of a competitive market come into play. Investments in the ICT capacities of the population also bring change slowly.

As with any other policy instruments, the pressure for delivery by both the political administration and the polity at large will be extremely high. A five-year delivery strategy does not fit within the political agenda of parties in government. What is more, experience shows that implementation of policy instruments that have a long timespan before delivery becomes demonstrable will lose impetus and political support, as attention will start to move towards other policy initiatives and changes in the socio-economic environment.

Both the strategy design and the process of e-government implementation will be modular in form and incremental in terms of implementation. The strategy, and future iterations of the strategy over the generational horizon, will ensure consistency and coherency as the process of e-government implementation proceeds over time.

Annex 5.1 Enterprise architecture frameworks

Zachman Enterprise Architecture Framework (EAF)

John Zachman is regarded as the person who introduced the idea of 'Information System Architecture' (ISA). He considered information system design by analogy to the work steps and the representations of the classical architect and producers of complex engineering products. When developing an IT system, it is obvious that many parties are involved. Business people have business requirements, which should be translated into ICT requirements and next be transformed into a combination of software and hardware that fulfils those requirements.

It is to be noted that Zachman EAF is not an information system architecture, but a set of such architectures. The Zachman EAF relies on the fact that architecture is relative to the perspective from which one looks at it, and to the question that is in mind when drawing the architecture. As such, the EAF presents two dimensions. The first dimension concerns the different perspectives of the different participants in the systems development process. The second dimension deals with the six basic English questions: what, how, where, who, when and why.

The Open Group Architecture Framework (TOGAF)

TOGAF is open standard, is governed by the OpenGroup and is not aligned with any technology or vendor. TOGAF is based on the US Department of Defence 'Technical Architecture for Information Management'. The first version was released in 1995 and it is currently at Version 9. It is directed to enable the design, evaluation and building of the right architecture for an organisation. There are four subset types of architecture in TOGAF: (i) the business (or business process) architecture – this defines the business strategy, governance, organisation and key business processes; (ii) the applications architecture – this kind of architecture provides a blueprint for the individual application systems to be deployed, their interactions and their relationships to the core business processes of the organisation; (iii) the data architecture – this describes the structure of an organisation's logical and physical data assets and data management resources; and (iv) the technology architecture – this describes the software infrastructure intended to support the deployment of core, mission-critical applications. This type of software is sometimes referred to as 'middleware'.

TOGAF has three key parts. First, the Architecture Development Method (ADM) – a series of phases which broadly outline the steps required to design and implement a typical IT solution. These range from initial concept through design, implementation and change management. Second, the Enterprise Continuum – assets that originate from the ADM and established industry standards (HTML, compliance, etc.). Third, the Resource Base – tools used to support the ADM cycle. These would include any architecture software systems used to manage the TOGAF process.

Service Oriented Architecture

The widespread emergence of the internet in the mid-1990s as a platform for electronic data distribution, along with the advent of structured information, revolutionised the ability to deliver information to any corner of the world. While the introduction of Extensible Mark-up Language (XML) as a structured format was a major enabling factor, the promise offered by SOAP- based web services (see Annex 5.2) triggered the discovery of architectural patterns that are now known as Service Oriented Architecture (SOA). Service Oriented Architecture is an architectural paradigm and discipline that may be used to build infrastructures enabling those with needs (consumers) and those with capabilities (providers) to interact via services across disparate domains of technology and ownership. Services act as the core facilitator of electronic data interchanges yet require additional mechanisms in order to function. Several new trends in the computer industry rely upon SOA as the enabling foundation. These include the automation of Business Process Management (BPM), composite applications (applications that aggregate multiple services to function) and the multitude of new architecture and design patterns generally referred to as Web 2.0.

Annex 5.2 Securing government interoperability[2]

Security

Security is critical for the success of e-government, as it enables trust and confidence in its services. In securing e-government, one must ensure data confidentiality, data integrity, citizen identification and non-repudiation. Thus, e-government raises transaction security concerns. The success of e-government, therefore, depends on the capability to guarantee that the transaction environment is available, reliable and secure.

A security framework for e-government can be categorised into three areas:

(i)   Citizen authentication and authorisation. This ensures citizen identification and non-repudiation.

(ii) Transaction transport security. This incorporates methods for securing data during transition to ensure data confidentiality and integrity.

(iii) Business continuity. These are the methods directed to ensure that the service is available even in the event of a non-planned shutdown.

Citizen authentication is the process of verifying and confirming the identity of the person accessing data or services. Authorisation is the process of allowing access to the data or services, controlled by the individual's access levels. Within an e-government framework, the users who will be using the services offered via the portal can assume one, or a combination, of the following three roles:

•   **Individual**: An individual can access data or services on his or her own behalf.

•   **Agent**: An agent is an individual or organisation that can access data or services on behalf of another individual/s or organisation/s provided that consent is granted to the agent by the data subject (individual or organisation).

•   **Organisational representative**: An organisational representative is an individual that can access data or services on behalf of an organisation(s) provided that consent is granted to the data subject (representative by the organisation).

The data and services to which an individual has access at any time while assuming any of the roles listed above will be determined by his or her profile, which will be maintained by a directory service. In view of this, and the nature of the data and services being offered within e-government, a four-level authentication model can be established (Figure 5.3). Different authentication levels will allow different user roles to access different services.

Table 5.1 Example of a four-tier authentication framework

No authentication	Data or services intended for the general public. No authentication should be required.	Viewing of an electronic document of a legislation
Restricted authentication	Documents or services of certain importance. A low level of authentication will be required to protect against misuse or loss (i.e. password).	Viewing of status of a particular court case
Confidential authentication	Personal documents or services affecting personal data. A higher level of authentication may be required to protect against significant problems or losses (i.e. password and pin code).	Viewing of social security benefits
Maximum authentication	Strictly confidential personal data or financial transactions. Full authentication may be required to protect personal safety and/or prevent considerable financial loss (i.e. digital certification).	Viewing personal medical records

Figure 5.3 Four-level authentication model

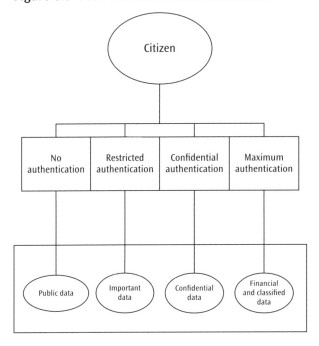

As data or personal information is passed from one entity to another via a medium, there is always the risk that this data is intercepted. Consequently, it may be stolen, misused, modified or denied (non-repudiation). This means that the confidentiality and integrity of the data will be jeopardised. As importantly, it may undermine trust and confidence in e-government.

Nevertheless, the level of security applied should reflect the degree of risk faced. The full approach of a digital certificate-based e-government security framework will be expensive to attain – both in terms of putting into place the appropriate technology and the procurement of necessary digital certificates, and also in the management and administration of the digital certificates.

Given the costs that would need to be financed balanced against the level of risk, the protection of the first three layers of the authentication model discussed above will constitute a high level of unnecessary engineering.

Thus, in tandem with the identification of the authentication model that one wishes to adopt, it is argued that it is of equal importance to determine the level of security to be applied for each e-service introduced. A digital certification security framework should be adopted only when the level of risk demands that the full protection armoury is to be applied, and always with regards to the use of sensitive personal data – such as health personal data.

Data interchange

Extensible Markup Language (XML) is a meta-language designed to create tags to define, transit, validate and interpret data. The use of XML-enabled middleware simplifies the development of data access components, especially when the number of data sources involved in data interchange increases

When the use of such middleware is deemed appropriate, systems should be designed with the use of these products in mind. The use of middleware conditions how data access components are designed and if a middleware product is introduced after a system is designed and developed, the data access components would need to be retrofitted – which would require unnecessary additional cost.

The purpose of an XML schema is to define and describe a class of XML documents by using the following constructs to constrain and document the meaning, usage and relationships of their constituent parts:

Data types   Provide for primitive data typing, including byte, date, integer, sequence etc.

Entities   An XML document may consist of one or many storage units, called entities. They all have content and are all identified by name.

Elements   An element can contain text, other elements, a mixture of text and elements, or nothing at all.

Attributes   Attributes are used to assign values to elements, including default values.

Notations   Notations identify by name the format of certain entities and elements, or the application to which a processing instruction is addressed.

Schema constructs may also provide for the specification of implicit information, such as default values. Schemas document their own meaning, usage and function. Thus, the XML schema language can be used to define, describe and catalogue XML vocabularies for classes of XML documents, sometimes referred to as 'instance documents'.

The following usage scenarios describe XML applications that should benefit from XML schemas. They represent a wide range of activities and needs that are representative of the problem space to be addressed. They are designed for use during the development of XML schemas, as design cases that should be reviewed when critical decisions are made.

1. **Publishing:** Distribution of information through publishing services. Involves collections of XML documents with complex relations among them. Structural schemas describe the properties of headlines, news stories, thumbnail images, cross-references etc.

2. **Electronic commerce transaction processing:** Libraries of schemas to define business transactions within markets and between parties. A schema-aware processor is used to validate a business document and to provide access to its information set.

3. **Supervisory control and data acquisition:** The management and use of network devices involves the exchange of data and control messages. Schemas can be used by a server to ensure the validity of outgoing messages, or by the client to allow it to determine what part of a message it understands. In a multi-vendor environment, the server discriminates data governed by different schemas (industry-standard, vendor-specific) and knows when it is safe to ignore information not understood and when an error should be raised instead. Applications include media devices, security systems and process control.

4. **Traditional document authoring and editing governed by schema constraints:** One important class of application uses a schema definition to guide an author in the development of documents. A simple example might be a memo, whereas a more sophisticated example is a complex request form. The application can ensure that the author always knows what to enter, and might even ensure that the data entered is valid.

5. **Query formulation and optimisation:** A query interface inspects XML schemas to guide a user in the formulation of queries. Any given database can emit a schema of itself to inform other systems what can be considered as legitimate and useful queries.

6. **Open and uniform transfer of data between applications and databases:** XML has become a widely used format for encoding data (including metadata and control data) for exchange between loosely coupled applications. The representation of the data exchange by XML schema definitions simplifies the task of mapping the data exchange to and from application internal data models.

7. **Metadata interchange:** There is growing interest in the interchange of metadata (especially for databases) and the use of metadata registries to facilitate inter-operability of database design as well as DBMS (data base management system), query, user interface, data warehousing and report generation tools.

Common government-wide business functions which make use of commonly used data should be encapsulated into business logic components that are common to all applications. This will facilitate the provision of integrated government services. For these components to be used to their maximum benefit, this exercise should be complemented by the production of XML-based data schemas relating to these common business functions.

These can be reused throughout government applications to reduce the costs and risks of developing data interchange systems. It is these common business functions which should be considered first for production of XML schemas.

Data architecture standards regarding the structure of the 'Person' and 'Address' entities, together with the validation rules that must be applied, should be designed within XML schemas. The design of such generic standards will enable enhanced data integration and exchange facilities through the use of agreed naming conventions and a mandatory record structure for the common data administration elements required in all data entities across all classifications.

This will result in a standardised data framework that will cut across all the administrative, corporate and function/service-specific data layers. Such a data architecture framework is intended to ensure that every item of data can be traced back to its author, the date and time, together with the business process triggering the update.

It will also create a standard security and access levels mechanism that can be used to filter records or individual attributes according to the authorisation held by the user. At the content level, other entities will be added to the government information-sharing platform where the data falls under public domain and the use of such data is considered critical for application integration purposes.

Component coupling and cohesion

Coupling refers to the way data is exchanged between components. Loose coupling is generally better than tight coupling. The loosest, and therefore preferred, type of coupling is data coupling, where data is transferred as parameters via well-defined interfaces. The tightest, or least desirable, coupling involves components directly referencing shared variables. Tight coupling often indicates that components are not insulated from one another, and are not designed to be separate and independent. Tightly coupled components are usually complex, difficult to maintain and monolithic. As a result there is very little flexibility regarding physical distribution of components. Two applications that communicate with each other via message queues, but which are otherwise independent of each other, would be considered loosely coupled.

Cohesion reflects the degree to which one component implements one function or a group of similar functions. For example, cohesive components do not implement multiple, disparate services, such as presentation and application logic. Highly cohesive components are typically more understandable and thus easier to maintain. Additionally, cohesion promotes logical and physical software distribution flexibility which, in turn, promotes system scalability. An application composed of logically separate presentation, application and data management components would be considered highly cohesive.

Software coupling and cohesion directly affect software modularity and interface design. As a result, coupling and cohesion directly affect the flexibility and complexity of software architectures. For example, when software component interfaces are based on widely accepted standards, as illustrated in Figure 5.4, logical software tiers can promote component interoperability and substitutability. That is, logical tiers can allow components within one tier to be changed without affecting other tiers.

Figure 5.4 Use of components in a typical three-tier architecture

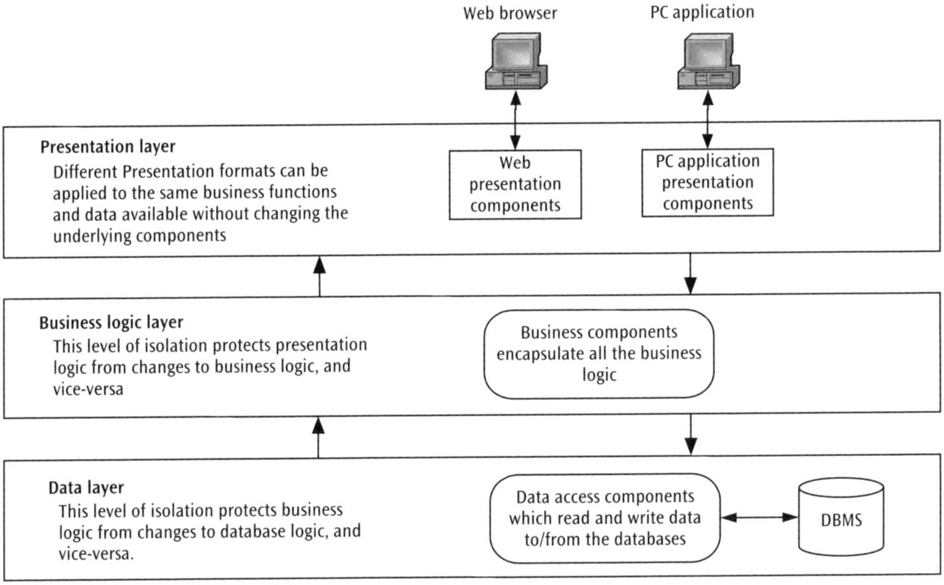

Message queuing

Message queuing enables distributed applications to reliably exchange mission-critical data regardless of hardware, operating system or available connectivity. Message queuing is roughly analogous to an email system. When an email message is sent, the note is addressed and sent to the intended recipients. One is not usually concerned about the underlying delivery route of the email message or when the recipients pick it up. Likewise, one can log into an email server and pick up messages at his or her discretion without maintaining a direct link with those who have sent the email.

Message queuing works in much the same manner as an email system, except that applications (not people) are sending data (not notes). Like email, the sending application does not have to be concerned about delivery routes or when the receiving application will pick up the message. The receiving application can pick up new messages whenever it is appropriate, without necessarily maintaining a direct link with the sending application.

Objects, components, services and e-services

The scene of application development has seen a transition of its design and development paradigms, from objects to components and, more recently, services and e-services. However, each remains a valid development solution, having benefits to give in different circumstances.

The design and development of systems should have, as their main focus, the provision of services. Service Oriented Architecture (SOA) has emerged as the best practice for systematic logical design of applications, offering greater reuse and more access to the business functions, or logical services, of the application from other applications. SOA is a logical architecture where definitive business functions of the application are exposed for programmatic access via a well-defined formal interface, with some means of identifying and locating the function and the interface when it is needed. SOA can be implemented both via a tightly coupled request/reply model and via a loosely coupled messaging model. It has also been implemented using either an object request broker (ORB) or messaging middleware. However, SOA services are typically intended for external (heterogeneous) access. Thus, the messaging model or messaging middleware are typically preferred for their implementation.

Each of these four programming styles may use either a tight or a loose coupling model. However, farther out along the x-axis (Figure 5.5), the link between programs typically becomes looser and the use of the loosely coupled messaging model and the messaging middleware become more beneficial. Conversely, if closer to the root of the diagram, it is more beneficial to use a tightly coupled request/reply programming model and ORB-style middleware.

Figure 5.5 Gartner development models for e-government services

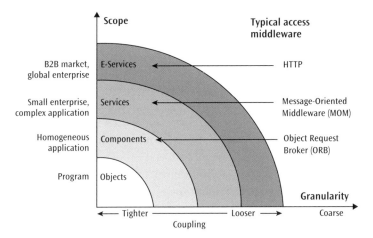

a) Objects

Objects are a natural evolution of the best programming practice: modularity. Long before object-oriented (OO) programming became mainstream, software engineers developed subroutines, Input/Output (I/O) modules and included files to encapsulate some of the application logic for reuse across the application or across applications.

The OO style of modularity is now mainstream. Most new applications are developed, at least in part, with the use of an OO programming platform (Java, C++ and Visual Basic). However, an object's scope of visibility is limited to the internal resources of a program, where it is instantiated. Object methods are invoked only from inside the program. Objects are incorporated inside the executable program so that the calling program and the object are more than tightly coupled, they are one.

b) Components

Scalable applications must be able to run across different servers. Thus, some of the methods may have to be invoked remotely. The caller and the server cannot be one in this case. To support remote invocation of object methods, the industry had invented ORBs. These programs, accessed via an ORB, are components.

The purpose of an ORB is to allow remote access to an object method with as little intrusion on the program or the programming model as possible. Thus, components are typically used in a tightly coupled, request/reply environment. This applies to all currently relevant component models, i.e., Distributed Component Object Model (DCOM), Common Object Request Broker Architecture (CORBA) and Java Remote Method Invocation (RMI).

The scope of components is bigger than that of objects, because they are visible to the remote programs. Many object methods are typically invoked on behalf of a single, remote procedure call (RPC). Components do not replace objects, but rather are built on top of them and component specifications are likely to support both the tightly coupled and the loosely coupled programming models.

It is a reality in application development that parts of applications will need to be rewritten because of changing requirements, legislation, changes in government policies etc. It is therefore very important to design components with business logic being kept separate from data access.

c)   Services

Services represent definitive published business functions of an application. They can be implemented using a tightly coupled request/reply programming model or a loosely coupled messaging programming model. Tightly coupled services operate just like components, but are published to a target audience potentially consisting of heterogeneous client platforms.

The loosely coupled services are designed differently, using the messaging model. Messaging is the preferred model for services, given that they are typically invoked from other applications. The greater the degree of heterogeneity, the more likely that a loosely coupled model would work better. Loosely coupled services are designed to operate independently of their callers. The corresponding applications may run on different machines, on different application platforms and in different geographical regions.

d)   e-Services

Business-to-business (B2B) interactions have become very important in today's information economies, in which both the business and technology differences are greater, the distances are longer and the possibilities for any co-ordination are further reduced.

Here, the program topology is likely to be loosely coupled in most cases. Enterprises are also not likely to have available the same proprietary messaging middleware. Thus, services offered across enterprises will tend to rely on existing messaging middleware and a standard method for formatting messages. Typically, this will be Extensible Markup Language (XML) messaging over HTTP or SMTP transports.

E-services are services deployed over a universal internet transport in an internet-standard format, such as XML over HTTP. Technically, any service may be converted to an e-service by routing it over HTTP and arranging the messages into an XML schema. Logically, however, e-services represent a separate domain of functional content, intended, authorised and advertised specifically for B2B access.

e) Simple Object Access Protocol (SOAP)

Simple Object Access Protocol (SOAP) allows the exchange of information in a decentralised, distributed environment using XML, making it usable in a large variety of systems, ranging from messaging systems to remote procedure calls (RPC). SOAP facilitates interoperability among a wide range of programs and platforms, making applications accessible to a broader range of users. It also combines the proven web technology of HTTP with the flexibility and extensibility of XML. Existing applications would need to be modified to accommodate this.

f) Universal Description, Discovery and integration (UDDI)

A 'web service' is a specific business functionality exposed by a company through an internet connection, for the purpose of providing a way for a third party to use the service. The Universal Description, Discovery and Integration (UDDI) specifications define a way to publish and discover information about web services. UDDI takes an approach that relies upon a distributed registry of businesses and their service descriptions implemented in a common XML format. Programs and programmers use the UDDI Business Registry to locate information about services and, in the case of programmers, to prepare systems that are compatible with advertised web services or to describe their own web services for others to call.

Notes

1   See CIMU 2000a.

2   Malta Information Technology and Training Services Ltd 2005.

References

Australian Government (1999), *Electronic Transactions Act 1999*, available at: www. comlaw.gov.au/Details/C2011C00445 (accessed 17 April 2013).

Central Information Management Unit (CIMU) (2000a), 'White Paper on the Vision and Strategy for e-Government', Office of the Prime Minister, Malta, October.

CIMU (2000b), 'White Paper on the Legislative Framework for Information Practices', Office of the Prime Minister, Malta, May.

EU (1995), 'Directive 95/46/EC of the European Parliament and of the Council of 24 October 1995, on the protection of individuals with regard to the processing of personal data and on the free movement of such data, Official Journal of the European Communities, No 281/31, 23/11/95, available at: http://ec.europa. eu/justice/policies/privacy/docs/95-46-ce/dir1995-46_part1_en.pdf (accessed 17 April 2013).

Germanakos, P, G Samaras and E Christodoulou (2004), 'Multi-channel delivery of services – the road from e-Government to m-Government: Further technological challenges and implications,' available at: http://www2.media.uoa.gr/~pgerman/ publications/published_papers/Multi-Channel_Delivery_of_eServices_from_ eGovt_to_mGovt.pdf (accessed 17 April 2013).

Government of Malta (2002), *Chapter 426: Electronic Commerce Act*, 10 May 2002, available at: http://intranet.stmartins.edu/courses/cis323/Resources/chapt426. pdf (accessed 17 April 2013).

Government of Sweden (1998), *Personal Data Act (1994:204)*, available at: www. sweden.gov.se/content/1/c6/01/55/42/b451922d.pdf (accessed 17 April 2013).

infoDev and ITU (2012), *Accountability, Transparency and Predictability*, ICT Regulation Toolkit, available at: www.ictregulationtoolkit.org/en/Documents.html (accessed 17 April 2013).

ISACA (2013), 'COBIT 5: A Business Framework for the Governance and Management of Enterprise IT', available at: www.isaca.org/COBIT/Pages/default.aspx (accessed 17 April 2013).

Malta Information Technology and Training Services Ltd. (2005), 'Interoperability Framework for e-Government', Office of the Prime Minister, Malta.

McCormick, KP (2013), 'Telecommunications Reform in Botswana: A Policy Model for African States', available at: www.sciencedirect.com (accessed 17 April 2013).

New Zealand State Services Commission (2008), *New Zealand E-Government Interoperability Framework*, available at: www.e.govt.nz/library/e-gif-v-3-3-complete. pdf (accessed 17 April 2013).

Office of the Attorney General (2000), *Irish Electronic Commerce Act, 2000*, Irish Statute Book, available at: www.irishstatutebook.ie/2000/en/act/pub/0027/print.html (accessed 17 April 2013).

United Nations (UN) (1999), *UNCITRAL Model Law on Electronic Commerce with Guide to Enactment 1996 with additional article 5 bis as adopted in 1998*, UN, New York, available at: www.uncitral.org/pdf/english/texts/electcom/05-89450_Ebook.pdf (accessed 17 April 2013).

United Nations Conference on Trade and Development (UNCTAD) (2003), *E-Commerce and Development Report 2003*, UNCTAD, New York and Geneva, available at: www.cnnic.net.cn/download/manual/international-report/edr03. pdf (accessed 17 April 2013).

United Nations Educational, Scientific and Cultural Organization (UNESCO) (2011), *UNESCO ICT in Education Policy Makers' Toolkit*, UNESCO Bangkok, available at: www.unescobkk.org/fr/education/ict/ict-in-education-projects/policy/toolkit (accessed 17 April 2013).

United States Government (2001), 'A Practical Guide to Federal Enterprise Architecture', Chief Information Officer Council, available at: www.gao.gov/ bestpractices/bpeaguide.pdf (accessed 17 April 2013).

Chapter 6

Emerging Directions in e-Government

Naveed Somani

This chapter looks at two recent developments in the area of e-government – mobile government and cloud computing – with a view to understanding how small states can utilise these technologies to enhance their ICT offerings now, or in the future.

Since the emergence of e-government in the late-1990s, citizens have become accustomed to being able to access government services electronically (Grönlund 2004). The dominant focus of governments in the last decade has been to automate government services to ensure they are suitable for an online environment, but strategies for service delivery have had a limited purview, neglecting numerous technology channels already harnessed by the private sector (Al-khamayseh et al. 2006). In particular, the rapid growth of wireless technologies in the developing world has exceeded that of wired line – especially in small states – obligating states to ensure mobile devices are considered as a necessary front-end delivery channel to access public services, reduce corruption and increase accountability. Mobiles have also proved a more attractive proposition for government from a financial perspective, with the infrastructure required to support their proliferation cheaper than fixed-line alternatives, and the multiple points of access contained in a single device – voice, SMS, MMS (multimedia messaging service) and broadband.

The need to reduce the capital costs associated with e-government has also led to the increased use of cloud services within both government and the private sector (KPMG 2012). While definitions vary, cloud computing aspires to reconceptualise the use of ICT systems in government as a utility cost that enables ubiquitous access to multiple applications, while reducing both the technical and human resources normally associated with e-government. The primary attraction for small states is that cloud technologies are elastic and can be scaled according to demand. The removal of large, up-front capital costs also ensures that government policy is not driven by long-term technology solutions to which states can sometimes become locked into. Furthermore, emerging standards on procurement and implementation should go some way to allay concerns around the outsourcing of ICT systems, particularly with regards to privacy and performance.

6.1 What is m-government?

M-government can be viewed as an extension, or supplement, to more traditional e-government models. The latter describes the use of wired technologies to facilitate the flow of information within and without public sector institutions to improve the efficiency, accountability and effectiveness of state services. Building on this definition, Kushchu and Kuscu define m-government as 'the utilization of all kinds of wireless and mobile technology, services, applications and devices for improving benefits to the parties involved in e-government including citizens, businesses and all government units' (2003). This definition presupposes the need for an e-government strategy, and in most cases countries are likely to utilise mobile devices as an alternate or extended delivery channel for services already offered via wired devices. However, e-government is not necessarily a prerequisite for m-government, particularly in the developing world where mobile phone penetration often far exceeds fixed-line infrastructure (ITU 2011). Mobile devices also offer a unique platform to go beyond the scope of what wired technologies can offer, for example in providing location-based services for emergency service professionals.

However, the mere automation of government services does not fully exploit the transformative potential these technologies offer. Mobile devices, if fully harnessed, can potentially facilitate a paradigm shift by enhancing the capacity of citizens to engage with government, thereby increasing social inclusion. The latter approach is better encapsulated under the term 'm-governance', which implies the potential to 'bring about a change in the way citizens relate to governments and to each other' (UNESCO 2005) and 'brings forth new concepts of citizenship, both in terms of citizen needs and responsibilities' (ibid). Ultimately, the 'objective is to engage, enable and empower the citizen' (ibid).

6.2 Why m-government?

The rationale for the development of m-government applications can be disaggregated as follows:

- **Accessibility:** Mobile phone penetration in the developing world has now reached 79 per cent, with twice as many mobile-broadband subscriptions as fixed-line connections – a contrast that becomes more acute when looking at coverage among rural populations (ITU 2011). With the advent of so called 'smart phones', users have multiple channels to access services – voice, text, video and web – and even older devices continue to be useful tools in improving governance. While internet-enabled devices are not as ubiquitous as traditional cell phones, penetration is increasing, with mobile-web subscriptions growing by 45 per cent over the last four years (ITU 2011). Penetration levels are likely to continue to increase, with the most significant future development being the growth of mobile broadband services, as potentially provided by third and fourth generation mobile

(3G, 4G) and its enhancements (Germanakos et al. 2005). The dissemination of these technologies represents a paradigm shift that has seen the emergence of new data services, combining the benefits of broadband with mobility. To ensure government services are truly inclusive it is therefore imperative that mobile delivery channels are fully exploited – even when this comes before the development of fixed-line services.

- **Affordability**: Mobile phone subscriptions in the developing world have fallen dramatically in cost over the last 10 years, with a 22 per cent fall between 2008 and 2010 alone (ITU 2011). Despite this fall, at 11.4 per cent of monthly gross national income (GNI) per capita, costs remain relatively high compared with only 2 per cent in developed countries (ibid). Nevertheless, compared with the high capital costs of infrastructure and devices associated with wired technologies, mobile technologies offer a significantly cheaper alternative for governments and users – particularly in countries with large distances between the location of the core infrastructural services and the outlying towns and communities, or which have a large rural community (Sciades et al. 2005). This cost efficiency equally applies to the development of mobile applications, which can be delivered with relatively little expense as opposed to more costly desktop solutions.

- **Mobility and personalisation**: Globalisation has meant people, objects and information have become increasingly mobile, with many now expecting delivery channels which fit in with their nomadic lifestyles (Vijayakumar et al. 2010) Wireless devices theoretically grant citizens access to government information and services 24/7 regardless of their environment. When allied with desktop services, this can be particularly useful in providing alerts or the equivalent service for a mobile device. Mobility also implies a potential change with regard to the physical location of the user, and the emergence of GPS has meant geography can be accounted for when personalising services, for example in reporting the location of a crime.[1]

- **Interactivity and participation**: Mobile technologies provide a new platform to facilitate interaction between government and citizens, which moves beyond the provision of transactional services such as e-payment applications. M-government has the potential to dramatically increase social inclusion by connecting government at the highest level with citizens previously excluded from participating due to the inaccessibility of traditional communication channels. Real-time mobile interaction also allows citizens to report immediately any instance of malfeasance on the part of government officials, thereby reducing corruption and improving efficiency. In widening the availability of channels for G2C and C2G interaction, citizen identification with the state is likely to improve, thus strengthening the social contract between state and citizen.

6.3 M-Government in small states

The introduction of low-cost mobile phone services more than a decade ago has transformed the telecommunications landscape, and increased access exponentially. Commonwealth small states in particular have witnessed dramatic rises in mobile tele-density, as reflected in Figure 6.1.

The figures for the Pacific region (Table 6.1) further emphasise the rapid growth in mobile cellular subscriptions. For example, in Papua New Guinea between

Figure 6.1 Mobile subscribers per 100 persons in Commonwealth African small states

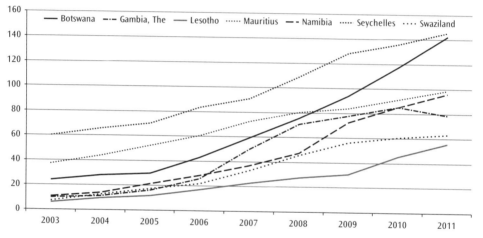

Source: World Bank, *World Development Indicators,* http://databank.worldbank.org

Figure 6.2   Mobile subscribers per 100 persons in Commonwealth Asian, Caribbean, European and Pacific small states

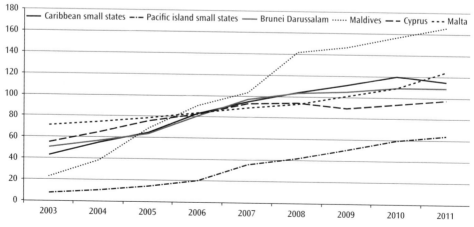

Source: World Bank, *World Development Indicators,* http://databank.worldbank.org

Table 6.1 Fixed telephone line and mobile subscribers per 100 persons in the Pacific

	Fixed telephone mainlines				Mobile cellular subscriptions						
	Per 100 population			% change per annum	Per 100 population			% change per annum	% of total subscribers		
	2000	2005	2009	05–09	2000	2005	2009	05–09	2000	2005	2009
Pacific	**39.6**	**36.8**	**31.8**	**–1.9**	**33.1**	**67.7**	**87.0**	**8.4**	**45.6**	**64.8**	**73.3**
American Samoa	17.9	16.5	15.5	0.0	3.5	3.5	–	–	16.3	17.5	–
Australia	52.4	49.6	41.2	–2.8	44.7	90.3	110.6	7.1	46.0	64.5	72.9
Cook Islands	32.0	34.0	34.2	1.1	3.4	20.6	34.7	15	9.5	37.7	50.4
Fiji	10.6	13.7	16.1	5.0	6.8	24.9	75.1	32.9	38.9	64.6	82.4
French Polynesia	22.6	21.0	20.3	0.4	16.8	47.1	77.8	14.8	42.6	69.2	79.3
Guam	48.0	38.9	36.9	0.0	17.5	58.1	–	–	26.8	59.9	–
Kiribati	4.0	4.6	4.1	–1.2	0.4	0.7	1.0	13.6	8.1	12.5	20.0
Marshall Islands	7.7	8.5	8.2	0.0	0.8	1.3	5.6	43.9	9.1	13.7	40.5
Micronesia (F.S.)	9.0	11.3	7.9	–8.5	0.0	12.9	34.3	28.1	0.0	53.2	81.4
Nauru	17.9	17.8	18.6	1.4	12.0	14.8	–	–	40.0	45.5	–
New Caledonia	24.1	23.9	27.3	5.1	23.5	58.1	84.9	11.8	49.5	70.8	75.7
New Zealand	47.5	41.8	43.3	2.0	40.0	85.4	108.7	7.4	45.7	67.1	71.5

(Continued)

Table 6.1 Fixed telephone line and mobile subscribers per 100 persons in the Pacific (cont.)

| | Fixed telephone mainlines | | | | Mobile cellular subscriptions | | | | | | |
| | Per 100 population | | | % change per annum | Per 100 population | | | % change per annum | % of total subscribers | | |
	2000	2005	2009	05–09	2000	2005	2009	05–09	2000	2005	2009
Niue	52.6	59.3	72.8	2.4	21.1	35.6	–	–	28.6	37.5	–
Northern Mariana Islands	30.7	34.6	40.8	1.9	4.4	30.4	–	–	12.5	46.8	–
Palau	–	40.2	34.9	-2.9	–	30.6	64.9	21.3	–	43.3	65.0
Papua New Guinea	1.2	1.0	0.9	-1.5	0.2	1.2	13.4	86.1	11.7	54.1	93.8
Samoa	4.8	10.8	17.5	13.1	1.4	13.3	82.8	58.4	22.7	55.2	82.6
Solomon Islands	1.9	1.6	1.6	2.6	0.3	1.3	5.7	49.5	13.5	44.8	78.5
Tonga	9.9	13.6	29.9	22.6	0.2	29.6	51.2	15.4	2.0	68.6	63.1
Tuvalu	7.4	9.3	17.3	17.2	0.0	13.4	20.4	11.4	0.0	59.1	54.1
Vanuatu	3.6	3.3	3.1	0.7	0.2	6.0	54.1	77.7	5.7	64.5	94.6

Source: UNESCAP 2011

2005–2009, mobile subscriptions increased by 86.1 per cent per year, compared to –1.5 per cent for fixed telephone lines. These figures have materialised despite mobile operators arriving much later to the state than their fixed-line counterparts, and the low levels of saturation for both types of service.

The increasing levels of mobile phone penetration not only present small states with an opportunity to implement m-government services generally, but also address the key challenges which hinder their development: human and institutional capacity; susceptibility to natural disasters, environmental change and income volatility; and issues of isolation and openness. Mobile devices have demonstrated their value as a medium uniquely placed to address these issues, for example in improving the pedagogy of pre-service teachers (Ferry 2009) and increasing access to financial services with mobile banking. SMS in particular has proved to be a vital tool in countering the effects of climate change, of which small states have witnessed its most deleterious consequences (Box 6.1).

Box 6.1 Trinidad and Tobago, SMS early warning

The Office of Disaster Preparedness and Management (ODPM) partnered with the Telecommunications Services of Trinidad and Tobago (TSTT) to establish an Emergency Short Message Service (ESMS) broadcasting agreement in 2010. In explaining the intricacies of this simple and effective message tool, the ODPM's Corporate Service Manager, Major Chevalier Jackson, reiterated that this service will be used to disseminate information on possible threats, impending hazardous events or any major crisis. Mobile phone owners typically carry their handsets with them, so these are a much more suitable means of relaying information instantly to those in harm's way, instead of relying on intermediaries such as television and radio which lack the advantages of mobility.

The effects of isolation have also had a largely negative impact, with domestic and international arbitrage proving to be an insidious force on economic development (Favaro 2008). The dissemination of market information to smooth these inequalities has been expedited by mobile phones, by, for example, communicating price fluctuations in agri-commodities to farmers (Jensen and Thysen 2003) Measures to support open government in small states can prove expensive to develop and maintain, particularly where data collection is required in support of open data initiatives (Farrugia 2006). In such instances, states should consider devising regional solutions, or pairing with intergovernmental organisations to exploit economies of scale. The World Bank, for example, is committed to ensuring small states maintain reliable data sets to assist in decision-making, but has also incorporated these statistics into its mobile open-data application, freely available for download.[2]

6.4 Implementing m-government

In introducing mobile solutions to service delivery, a sequential approach is needed to ensure sustainability and foster trust among users. The various stages of m-government from 'Push' to 'Participatory' can be seen in Figure 6.3, which illustrates a suggested trajectory states may wish to adopt, with corollary examples from across the Commonwealth.

6.5 Adoption factors

In moving up through the stages of m-government, states should adopt a strategic approach which outlines a coherent path, integrated across all government ministries. This can be achieved as part of a broader e-government strategy, or may be stand alone while allowing for the eventual incorporation into a wider ICT strategy. Regardless of which approach is taken, m-government should not be considered in isolation of any general discussions on service delivery generally, but rather as an additional channel available to government. It is also imperative that policy-makers place the requirements of their citizens at the forefront of their minds in developing applications (Hellstrom 2009). The 'Design-Reality' gap (Heeks 2003) has been cited as the primary reason for the failure of e-government projects, so governments should not only ensure products are addressing an identified need, but also fully comprehend the resource requirements necessary to develop notional ideas. A summary of the key adoption factors states should consider can be seen in Table 6.2.

Table 6.2 Key adoption factors for m-government

National-level policies	Socio-cultural	Technological	Economic
Fostering sufficient political support, with corollary human and financial resources identified Building ICT competencies within government Development of standards in mobile sector Development of a 'whole of government' m-government strategy	Bespoke content development appropriate for devices and end users, given country context – i.e. location, demographics, literacy levels, accessibility requirements Building competencies in the use of mobile ICTs	Infrastructure necessary for the use of mobile devices: base stations, WAP servers, GPRS Support Node Device and application development	Removal of tariff/non-tariff barriers to ICT products Formation of multi-stakeholder partnerships including telecommunications companies, government, regulators, device manufacturers, infrastructure providers, citizen groups and application developers Measures to align purchasing power and cost of mobile devices

Source: Adapted from Dholakia and Kshetri 2001

Figure 6.3 Stages of m-government

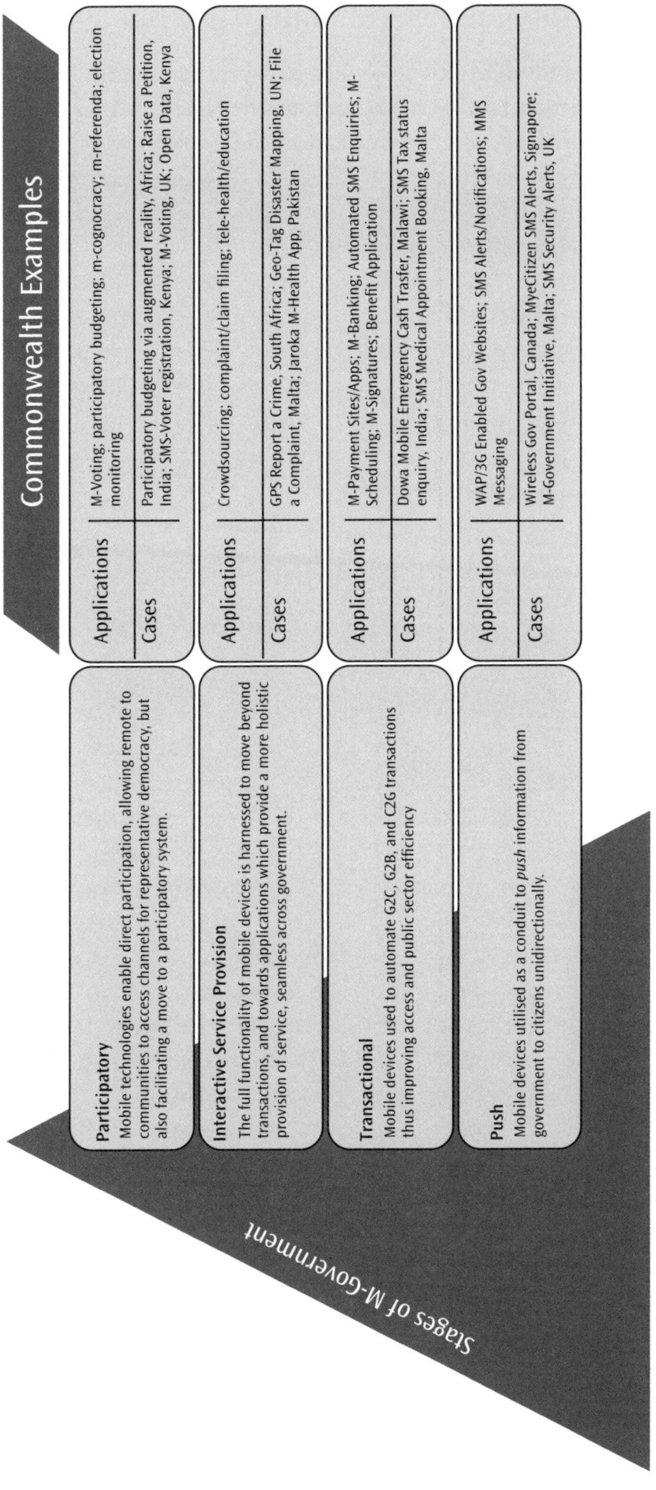

	Commonwealth Examples
Participatory Mobile technologies enable direct participation, allowing remote to communities to access channels for representative democracy, but also facilitating a move to a participatory system.	**Applications**: M-Voting; participatory budgeting; m-cognocracy; m-referenda; election monitoring
	Cases: Participatory budgeting via augmented reality, Africa; Raise a Petition, India; SMS-Voter registration, Kenya; M-Voting, UK; Open Data, Kenya
Interactive Service Provision The full functionality of mobile devices is harnessed to move beyond transactions, and towards applications which provide a more holistic provision of service, seamless across government.	**Applications**: Crowdsourcing; complaint/claim filing; tele-health/education
	Cases: GPS Report a Crime, South Africa; Geo-Tag Disaster Mapping, UN; File a Complaint, Malta; Jaroka M-Health App. Pakistan
Transactional Mobile devices used to automate G2C, G2B, and C2G transactions thus improving access and public sector efficiency	**Applications**: M-Payment Sites/Apps; M-Banking; Automated SMS Enquiries; M-Scheduling; M-Signatures; Benefit Application
	Cases: Dowa Mobile Emergency Cash Trasfer, Malawi; SMS Tax status enquiry, India; SMS Medical Appointment Booking, Malta
Push Mobile devices utilised as a conduit to *push* information from government to citizens unidirectionally.	**Applications**: WAP/3G Enabled Gov Websites; SMS Alerts/Notifications; MMS Messaging
	Cases: Wireless Gov Portal, Canada; MyeCitizen SMS Alerts, Signapore; M-Government Initiative, Malta; SMS Security Alerts, UK

Stages of M-Government

6.6 Financing m-government: multi-stakeholder partnerships

Locating sufficient funding for m-government initiatives can ultimately determine whether fledgling projects get off the ground or not. Funding arrangements should not only consider capital costs and infrastructure development, but also the technical resources required to maintain applications and financial commitments for future development. Public–private partnerships (PPPs) are often an attractive model for governments, with several successful examples already well established.[3] However, there exists an inherent conflict in partnering with the private sector, with many operators, who thus far have driven the development of mobile applications, motivated by either profit or brand enhancement via corporate social responsibility programmes (Hellström 2010). States should consider the role of multi-stakeholder partnerships in resolving this conflict, a model that not only includes the public and private sectors, but also representation from civil society. Unlike PPPs, they focus on sharing, rather than shifting risks, and exploit synergies to deliver mutual benefits for all collaborating parties. The Global Knowledge Partnership has described them as, 'Alliances between parties drawn from government, business and civil society that strategically aggregate the resources and competencies of each to resolve the key challenges of ICT as an enabler of sustainable development, and which are founded on principles of shared risk, cost and mutual benefit' (2003). It is a model that has seen success in various sector-specific e-government initiatives,[4] and could easily be applied in the development of m-government services.

Balancing the need for novel approaches to e-government with the costs accrued in procuring new technologies is a constant challenge, particularly in an environment where any new investment by government is closely scrutinised. Cloud computing claims to offer a solution in that it grants access to new applications as and when required, while also reducing the capital outlay normally associated with IT procurement. Cloud services are already ubiquitous in the private sector, with governments now seeking to harness their benefits for use in improving public administration. For small states, these benefits go directly towards addressing the challenges they face – human and institutional capacity; susceptibility to natural disasters, environmental change and income volatility; and issues of isolation and openness – but where internet access remains intermittent, holistic cloud solutions are likely to remain a technology for the future.

6.7 What is cloud computing?

Cloud computing is an emerging concept, encompassing nomenclature previously associated with terms defined separately (Figure 6.4). Definitions of cloud computing vary (Wyld 2009), but the one most often adopted by government comes from the US government's National Institute of Standards and Technology (NIST) which states that, 'Cloud computing is a model for enabling ubiquitous, convenient, on-demand

Figure 6.4   Concept of cloud computing

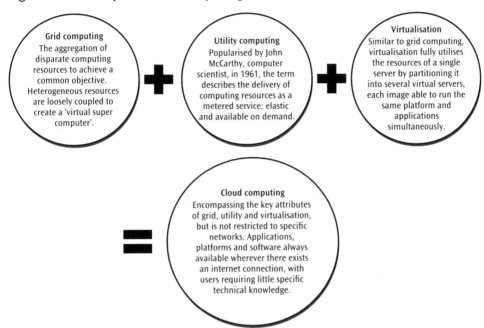

network access to a shared pool of configurable computing resources (e.g., networks, servers, storage, applications, and services) that can be rapidly provisioned and released with minimal management effort or service provider interaction' (Mell and Grance 2009).

Depending on the specific requirements of the users, cloud computing can be further disaggregated as follows:

- Software as a Service (SaaS): The client identifies the applications required, and the vendor ascertains the resources needed to meet anticipated demand. The vendor retains control of the infrastructure and operating system, with the client gaining access to the application locally.

- Platform as a Service (PaaS): The clients gain access to a hosting environment in which they can design, implement and deploy web applications and services. No software download is required, and the vendor retains control over the operating system, hardware and network infrastructure.

- Infrastructure as a Service (IaaS): The client gains access and control over infrastructure in the form of a virtual environment. From the client's perspective it is *tabula rasa* (blank slate), though they do not, in fact, have control over any physical infrastructure, rather virtualised storage, networks and process power, which in reality are running concurrently to other virtual environments.

For small states no one particular service model holds increased appeal. Nevertheless, when arriving at a decision factors such as security, privacy, knowledge retention (i.e. the ability to bring services in-house) and cost should be balanced appropriately.

Figure 6.5 illustrates the four deployment models available to government.

Government agencies have to reconcile their need to accommodate both business-critical private data with information designed for public consumption. For this reason, hybrid clouds are finding favour over public or private solutions. Hybrid platforms meet the stringent security needs of government, but also deliver the benefits associated with public access models, i.e. scalability and cost savings.

Large federal governments, in recognition of their size and breadth, have deployed their cloud technologies on a community cloud basis – despite the constituent entities not being strictly delineated (McEvoy and Koop 2008). Community clouds better reflect the emerging paradigm of 'Digital-era Governance' (DEG), which scholars argue has replaced 'New Public Management' as the dominant focus for public administration (Dunleavy et al. 2006). In contrast to Weberian disaggregation, cloud technologies contribute to a key tenet of DEG, namely reintegration and the de-silo process, with community clouds in particular drawing on synergies between disparate government agencies to re-governmentalise issues of inherent concern to the state (ibid).

Figure 6.5 Cloud deployment models

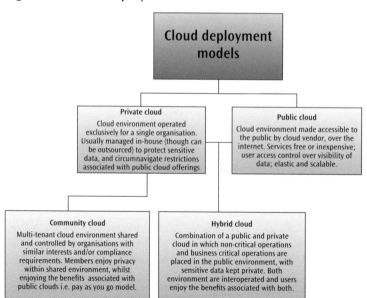

Given the opportunity to access services via remote data centres, and the need to maximise cost savings, small states should consider a regional community-hybrid approach, whereby non-sensitive services such as payroll applications are purchased collectively with other neighbouring islands, while business-critical applications are purchased at the state level.

6.8 Why cloud computing?

The public sector lends itself to the use of cloud technology in that it contains similar organisational and functional units (Cellary and Strykowski 2009). For example, police stations in a single sovereign territory will be subject to the same legal and operational requirements. Cloud technology can house applications useful to all such units in a single container, accessed as a service by geographically disparate police stations. Metadata from individual units can also be collected, which allow for the modification of software to create bespoke solutions according to the requirements communicated. Governments also require similar functions to be performed across all its units (e.g. procurement or payroll) and here the cloud would operate in a similar manner (ibid) (Figure 6.6).

Figure 6.6 Similar functional units' access to government cloud

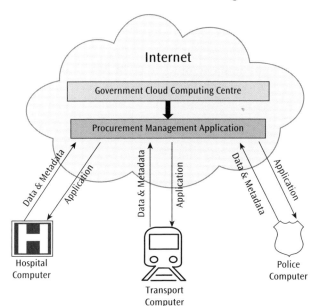

In addition, cloud computing confers the following benefits:

- **Elasticity.** Cloud computing's primary appeal is that it reconceptualises the procurement of IT resources as a utility, allowing governments to scale resources up or down as required: instead of capital investment in infrastructure and software, governments purchase access to remote, location independent computing resources via a ubiquitous area network, i.e. the internet. The cloud vendor would then invoice the government either on a subscription basis or, in common with other utilities, on a pay-as-you-go basis.

- **Cost savings.** In comparison to the traditional provision of IT services, the move towards cloud solutions offers significant cost reductions. Apart from the savings conferred by elasticity, maintenance and administration costs are reduced due to the decreased need for highly trained staff (a benefit for small states, in particular, where human capital is low); resources normally dedicated to maintaining traditional IT systems are freed up, thereby increasing productivity; and the aggregation of resources dedicated to servicing larger units of government reduces the cost of maintaining separate iterations of similar applications.

- **Ubiquitous access.** Untethered from using individual, usually wired, hardware, civil servants can access applications and documents from any location with internet access (including properly secured and encrypted mobile devices). The consolidation of services also improves citizen access to e-government applications.

- **Green cloud.** Utilised correctly, cloud technology has the potential to reduce the carbon footprint of government. This reduction is achieved largely by consolidating data centres; making cooling systems more efficient; virtualising physical storage; and reducing power usage (Rouse 2011).

- **Improved disaster recovery.** Cloud vendors offer various cost-effective services for recovering data, applications and operating systems. For small states where natural disasters are increasing in frequency this is particular important. Services include the provision of duplicate cloud infrastructure supplied by the vendor to migrate to in the event of a disaster, and subscription services such as access to the cloud environment at designated data centres.

- **Service quality and security.** The onus to ensure uptime, and apply patches and updates, is shifted to the cloud vendor. Implementation time for new solutions, particularly in response to changes in regulations, is reduced.

- **Diffusion of best practice.** For larger countries, the move to the cloud ensures that modern technology is accessible even at the lowest levels of government. Good practices are often hermetically sealed in organisational silos, but cloud architecture encourages the dissemination of best practice across all units of government. Uniformity in e-government not only reduces cost, but improves 'brand identity' with the public. A consistent approach also contributes to a 'whole of government' e-government strategy, essential for the successful integration of IT in public service delivery (UNDESA 2012). For small states, as cloud computing is increasingly integrated in governments around the world, they are likely to benefit from the institutional knowledge accumulated by service providers.

- **'Big Data' analysis.** An issue for larger rather than small states, 'Big Data' describes the large amount of unstructured data countries accumulate in the course of their business. These data sets can be mined to identify trends that can potentially contribute to improved service delivery and economic development, but due to their size are too costly to analyse. Cloud vendors have the ability to pool resources to provide sufficient computational power to analyse Big Data sets in real time (NIST 2012).

6.9 Key adoption factors

| NATIONAL-LEVEL POLICIES | **Development of a cloud migration strategy** (Figure 6.7)

The revision of procurement guidelines: The cloud market is relatively immature and approaches to procurement are inconsistent across governments. Several have separated the purchasing of cloud technology from their core procurement practices, instead developing 'cloud stores' from which agencies can buy cloud applications (Hodgkinson 2012). This model has yet to show success, however, and what appears to be more important is that government agencies have sufficient information to understand their IT needs, enabling them to 'shop' for cloud solutions intelligently (ibid).

Establishment of a legal and regulatory environment: The ITU has published a comprehensive list of recommendations for cloud regulation that are applicable universally (ITU 2012). In summary, these recommendations require legislation to cover 'the transposition to the national level of subregional, regional or international texts on data protection; revision of relevant legislation to take account of the status of cloud-hosted data; strengthening of legislation, codes of conduct and standards applicable to the ICT sector; and clarification of relations between data centre managers, cloud computing and data protection' (ibid: pviii). |
| HUMAN RESOURCES | **Building ICT competencies:** Cloud applications are generally designed so as to require only minimal ICT skills on the part of the user, and with resources outsourced to the cloud fewer technicians are needed to maintain infrastructure. Nevertheless, civil servants and citizens alike need to be sensitised to the new ICT environment, and trained in new skills where necessary.

Bespoke content development: Similar to m-government, local developers should be empowered to develop content suitable for the domestic market. Focus groups should be utilised where possible to ensure content and applications meet an identified need. |

(Continued)

HUMAN RESOURCES (cont.)	**Fostering a collaborative environment:** Cloud computing encourages uniformity in e-government across all units of government, and with that comes new opportunities for collaboration. Governments should not only ensure applications encourage joint working and the sharing of data, but foster a silo-busting collaborative environment.
TECHNOLOGICAL	**Reliable network access:** For small states, this remains the biggest obstacle to the implementation of cloud services. Reliable and readily available internet access is essential if governments are to realise the economic and technological benefits of the cloud.
	Cloud security: This is a concern that in reality requires a multifaceted solution encompassing not only technological safeguards, but also robust legal mechanisms and suitable training for staff. Any security policy should be designed to ensure compliance with regulation; protect data, information, applications and infrastructure; safeguard privacy; and contain a business continuity and backup plan in case of a security breach. Depending on the deployment model selected, multi-tenancy can pose a significant risk to any government contracted to a cloud vendor (Subashini and Kavitha 2011). Public clouds are the least secure in this regard, as several subscribers may be sharing a single machine, each of which represent a potential security risk. Hybrid clouds technically allow for data to be stored in locations appropriate to their sensitivity, but governments should pre-agree a policy on 'cloud-bursting' – where an application contained within the private cloud requires extra computing resources and 'bursts' into the public cloud – with their vendor (Badger and Grance 2010).
	The NIST has developed security standards which provide guidance as to how and where applications should be stored depending on the sensitivity of the information collected (Barker 2003). Where data is highly sensitive – for example, where it pertains to national security – it should be stored in a private cloud, owned and maintained in country. However, this is expensive and states should therefore be cognisant of the costs and benefits of different security decisions. Costs should also be shared appropriately between the contracting state and cloud vendor, without compromising security. Where possible states should develop a certification system awarded to suppliers that meet stringent security standards (KPMG 2012).
ECONOMIC	**Return on Investment (ROI):** To realise the savings associated with moving with the cloud, governments must engage in complex ROI analysis. When approaching this task, governments should ensure that benefits obtained from moving to the cloud, e.g. reduced risk profile or improved functionality, are costed and netted from investment costs to obtain a more accurate ROI profile. Other factors that affect ROI include human resource costs; infrastructure savings; improvements in speed; costs of the green cloud; changes in software; and future cost implications (i.e. falling cost of the cloud vs. rising cost of maintaining internal ICT assets). Metrics that governments may find useful include: 'Discounted Payback Period', 'Benefit-to-Cost Ratio', and 'Net Present Value' (Jackson 2009).

Figure 6.7 Cloud migration strategy

1 Learning

Policy-makers educated on the merits and demerits of cloud computing by technical staff. Research conducted on the state of cloud computing to understand risks and rewards.

2 Organisational Assessment

Establish current ICT baselines looking at need, demand and resources utilisation. This should inform decisions on whether cloud resources are necessary to meet current requirements or can be contracted as and when extra resources are required.

3 Cloud Pilot

IT professionals develop a cloud computing pilot based on the requirement for the particular project. 'Rogue' projects conducted by individual agencies should also be encouraged as learning from these can assist in establishing best practice, and also drive the eventual adoption of cloud technologies.

4 Cloud Assessment

Assessment of which existing applications and data can easily be migrated to the cloud, and selection of deployment model. Applications and data which should not be migrated are also identified.

5 Cloud Rollout Strategy

Cloud integrated a part of existing operations, and rolled out across government. Buy in sought from all layers of government, and stakeholders informed of change in IT infrastructure, and the corollary benefits.

6 Continuous Improvement

Data and applications continually assessed for their suitability for the cloud, and migrated accordingly. Policy-makers respond to emerging developments e.g. variable user credentials.

6.10 Cloud migration

The move to the cloud should contribute to achieving the goals already laid out in an e-government strategy. For this reason leadership is paramount, as an overarching view is required to ensure cloud technologies meaningfully contribute to a holistic and consistent view of e-government. A top-down approach is therefore required, and the migration process should focus on eliminating redundancy; ensuring interoperability; and harmonising processes regardless of technology. IT professionals have devised a six-step 'cloud migration strategy' for governments considering moving their IT assets to a cloud environment (Wyld 2010) (Figure 6.7).

6.11 Mobility now, cloud later

Given the high and ever-increasing penetration levels of mobile subscribers in small states, m-government can no longer be regarded as an option for the future by government policy-makers. However, the technological and regulatory requirements associated with the government cloud do make it an option for the future. Once universal and 'always-on' internet is achieved, and the cloud market has matured, the adoption of cloud services in small states represents a genuine opportunity for them to offer the full panoply of e-government services otherwise found in much larger countries. These challenges are not common to all small states, however, and where there is an opportunity to move to the cloud, countries should consider working with regional organisations to deploy applications via a community-hybrid cloud.

Notes

1   Citizens in South Africa can report the location of a crime using GPS as part of the wider 'Turn it Around' project. See: www.turnitaround.co.za/report_a_crime (accessed 21 December 2012).

2   See: http://blogs.worldbank.org/opendata/mobile-apps-for-health-jobs-and-poverty-data (accessed 11 November 2012).

3   For example, South Africa's 'Turn it Around' project. See note 1.

4   For example, DFID's Imfundo Programme aims to create partnerships to contribute to the delivery of universal primary education and gender equality in Africa through the use of ICTs. See: http://webarchive.nationalarchives.gov.uk/+/www.dfid.gov.uk/research/imfundo.asp (accessed 21 December 2012).

References

Al-Khamayseh, Shadi and Elaine Lawrence (2006), 'Towards citizen centric mobile government services: a roadmap.' *CollECTeR Europe 2006*: 129.

Badger, L and T Grance (2010), 'Standards Acceleration to Jumpstart Adoption of Cloud Computing (SAJACC),' *Presentation at the 2010 National Institute of Standards and Technology [NIST] Cloud Computing Workshop*, Gaithersburg, Maryland, USA, May.

Barker, W (2003), *Guide for mapping types of information and information systems to security categories, ITL Bulletin* [online newsletter], July, Gaithersburg, Maryland, USA.

Cellary, W and S Sergiusz (2009), 'E-government based on cloud computing and service-oriented architecture', *Proceedings of the Third International Conference on Theory and Practice of Electronic Governance*, ACM Press, New York, USA.

Dholakia, N and N Kshetri (2001), 'The Global Digital Divide and Mobile Business Models: Identifying Viable Patterns of e-Development', University of Rhode Island, USA.

Dunleavy, P, H Margetts, S Bastow, and J Tinkler (2006), 'New public management is dead—long live digital-era governance', *Journal of Public Administration Research and Theory*, 16(3), 467–494.

Farrugia, N (2006), *Institution-Building with a Focus on Small States*, Global Development Network.

Favaro, EM (Ed.) (2008), *Small States, Smart Solutions: Improving Connectivity and Increasing the Effectiveness of Public Services*, World Bank, Washington, DC.

Ferry, B (2009), 'Using mobile phones to enhance teacher learning in environmental education', in J Herrington, A Herrington, J Mantei, I Olney, B Ferry (Eds.) *New Technologies, New Pedagogies: Mobile Learning in Higher Education*, University of Wollongong, Wollongong, 45–55.

Germanakos, P, S George and C Eleni (2005), 'Multi-channel Delivery of Services – the Road from eGovernment to mGovernment: Further Technological Challenges and Implications', *Proceedings of the First European Conference on Mobile Government (Euro mGov 2005)*.

Global Knowledge Partnership (2003), 'Multi-stakeholder Partnerships: Issue Paper', Knowledge for Development Series, available at: www.odi.org.uk/resources/docs/2117.pdf (accessed 17 July 2012).

Grönlund, A (2004), 'Introducing e-Gov: History, Definitions, and Issues', *Communications of the Association for Information Systems*, Vol. 15, 713–729.

Heeks, R (2003), 'Most eGovernment-for-Development Projects Fail: How Can Risks be Reduced?', *Paper 14, i-Government Working Paper Series*, Institute for Development Policy and Management, University of Manchester, UK.

Hellström, J (2009), 'Mobile phones for good governance – challenges and way forward', Draft discussion paper, *World Wide Web Consortium*, March, available at: www.w3.org/2008/10/MW4D_WS/papers/hellstrom_gov.pdf (accessed 30 August 2012).

Hellström, J (2011), 'What evidence exists to support the argument that the mobile phone is an effective tool in the fight against corruption?', *Spider – The Swedish Program for ICT in Developing Regions Newsletter* Vol. 24, 12 September 2011, available at: http://spider.dsv.su.se/news/what-evidence-exists-support-argument-mobile-phone-effective-tool-fight-against-corruption (accessed 17 September 2012).

Hodgkinson, S (2012), 'Government cloud: agencies need shopping skills, not just cloud stores', *Ovum View* [blog], 19 December, available at: http://ovum.

com/2012/12/19/government-cloud-agencies-need-shopping-skills-not-just-cloud-stores/ (accessed 21 December 2012).

International Telecommunication Union (2011), 'The world in 2011: ICT facts and figures' [online], available at: www.itu.int/ITU-D/ict/facts/2011/material/ICTFactsFigures2011.pdf (accessed 3 September 2012).

International Telecommunications Union (2012), *Cloud computing in Africa: Situation and perspectives*, United Nations, Geneva.

Jackson, K (2009), 'Government Cloud Computing.' Dataline LLC, Virginia, USA.

Jensen, AL and I Thysen (2003), 'Agricultural information and decision support by SMS', *Proceedings of EFITA 2003*, Debrecen, Hungary.

KPMG (2012), *Exploring the Cloud: A Global Study of Governments' Adoption of Cloud*, KPMG International Cooperative.

Kushchu, I and H Kuscu (2003), 'From E-Government to M-Government: Facing the Inevitable', in the Proceedings of *European Conference on E-Government ECEG 2003*, Trinity College, Dublin.

McEvoy, N and D Koop (2011), *Government Community Cloud: Driving cost reduction through Shared Service Cloud Centres*, Cloud Best Practices, available at: http://cloudbestpractices.files.wordpress.com/2011/08/government-community-cloud.pdf, (accessed 19 November 2012).

Mell, P and T Grance (2009), *NIST definition of cloud computing*, National Institute of Standards and Technology, Washington, DC.

National Institute of Standards and Technology (2012), 'Cloud Computing and Big Data Intersect at NIST', *Tech Beat* [online newsletter], 29 November 2012, Available at: www.nist.gov/itl/math/cloud-112912.cfm (accessed 21 December 2012).

Rouse, M (updated August 2011), *DEFINITION Green Cloud* [online], available at: http://searchcloudstorage.techtarget.com/definition/green-cloud (accessed 15 November 2012).

Sciades, G (Ed.) (2005), *From the Digital Divide to Digital Opportunities: Measuring infostates for Development*, ITU/Orbicom, Montreal.

Subashini, S and V Kavitha (2011), 'A survey on security issues in service delivery models of cloud computing', *Journal of Network and Computer Applications*, Vol. 34 No. 1, 1–11.

UN Economic, Scientific and Cultural Organization (UNESCO) (2005), *Defining E-Governance* [online], available at: http://portal.unesco.org/ci/en/ev.phpURL_ID=4404&URL_DO=DO_TOPIC&URL_SECTION=201.html (accessed 19 September 2012).

United Nations Department of Economic and Social Affairs (2012), *United Nations E-Government Survey*, United Nations, New York.

United Nations Economic and Social Commission for Asia and the Pacific (UNESCAP) (2011), *Statistical Yearbook for Asia and the Pacific 2011*, United Nations, Thailand.

Vijayakumar, S, K Sabarish and G Krishnan (2010), 'Innovation and M-Governance: The Kerala Mobile governance experience and road-map for a comprehensive m-governance strategy'. *In W3C (World Wide Web Consortium), 20th International World Wide Web Conference*, Hyderabad, India, 28 March–1 April 2011. Kerala State IT Mission.

Wyld, D (2009), *Moving to the Cloud: An Introduction to Cloud Computing in Government*, IBM Center for the Business of Government, Washington, DC.

Wyld, D (2010), 'The cloudy future of government IT: Cloud computing and the public sector around the world', *International Journal of Web and Semantic Technology* Vol. 8 No. 9, 1–20.